SIX MILLION ANGELS

CHARLES COLSON AND MARK EARLEY
present

SIX
MILLION
Angels

Stories From 20 Years of Angel Tree's Ministry
to the Children of Prisoners

SERVANT PUBLICATIONS
ANN ARBOR, MICHIGAN

Vine Books is an imprint of Servant Publications especially designed to serve evangelical Christians.

Servant Publications—Mission Statement

We are dedicated to publishing books that spread the gospel of Jesus Christ, help Christians to live in accordance with that gospel, promote renewal in the church, and bear witness to Christian unity.

All Scripture quotations, unless indicated, are taken from the HOLY BIBLE, NEW INTERNATIONAL VERSION®. Copyright 1973, 1978, 1984 by International Bible Society. Used by permission of Zondervan Publishing House. All rights reserved.

Published by Servant Publications
P.O. Box 8617
Ann Arbor, Michigan 48107
www.servantpub.com

Cover design: Alan Furst, Minneapolis, Minn.

03 04 05 06 10 9 8 7 6 5 4 3 2 1

Printed in the United States of America
ISBN 1-56955-387-4

Library of Congress Cataloging-in-Publication Data

Six million angels : stories from 20 years of Angel Tree's ministry to
the children of prisoners / [edited by] Charles Colson and Mark Earley.
     p. cm.
 ISBN 1-56955-387-4 (alk. paper)
 1. Church work with children of prisoners. 2. Prison Fellowship. I.
Colson, Charles W. II. Earley, Mark. III. Prison Fellowship.
 BV4464.2.S59 2003
 259'.5–dc21

                                                      2003008406

$\mathcal{A}$CKNOWLEDGMENTS

This book is dedicated to the glory of God and to *every* person, on earth or in heaven, who has participated in the Angel Tree program.

The stories collected in this book were written over the years by the following Prison Fellowship writers:

Tamela Baker
Becky Beane
Evelyn Bence
David Carlson
Katherine Craddock
Ron Humphrey
Jeanette Nagel
Jeff Peck
John Shaw
Ellen Vaughn
Tawnia Wheeler

Special thanks to Ron Humphrey, a man whose love for Angel Tree knows no bounds, and in whose heart this book was born some two years ago. Thanks also to Evelyn Bence for her editorial hand in structuring the book. Finally, thanks to John Dawson and Alan Terwilleger of Prison Fellowship and Bert Ghezzi of Servant Publications for their commitment to have these stories told.

David Carlson
Vice-President, Ministry Communications
Prison Fellowship

Contents

PREFACE
BY CHARLES W. COLSON

In 1974 when I pled guilty to a Watergate offense and was escorted to Maxwell Federal Prison Camp in Alabama, I took on a new identity. I was not Mr. Colson, private citizen, with a standard-issue Social Security number. I was not a U.S. Marine, with a proudly worn dog tag. I was not a presidential assistant with a top-secret security clearance. I was a convicted felon, a menace to the public welfare.

As jarring and painful as my prison term was to me, in Maxwell my sleepless nights were not caused by the personal restrictions and indignities of my confinement. As a new Christian, I was willing to accept responsibility for my actions. No, my worries revolved around my family—knowing how my conviction had disrupted their lives and disturbed *their* self-identities. Maybe you know that feeling: that it's easier to trust God to take care of yourself than of your children.

What I felt and saw in prison changed the course of my life and led to God's call to establish Prison Fellowship Ministries, which at first focused on discipling Christian prisoners—strengthening and helping them live out their faith. But soon the ministry's vision broadened—to help the church show the love of Christ and communicate the gospel to all prisoners and ex-prisoners ... and their families.

My ears perked up in the mid-1980s at our annual staff retreats; I noticed an escalating excitement about a new aspect of ministry—helping prisoners connect with their children. *Yes!* I thought. *Skeptical prisoners will take notice if Christians help them help their children.*

They have—as is obvious in the stories throughout this book.

But that open door to the gospel is only the beginning of the astounding worldwide ministry of Angel Tree. Volunteers giving Christmas gifts to children on behalf of an imprisoned parent. Estranged family members finding one another—and God. Churches welcoming prisoners' families into their midst. Children receiving attention and life-lessons from mentors. Kids finding wholesome adventure at summer camp. Ex-prisoners finding joy in grateful generosity to a younger generation of prisoners' children—Angel Tree children, whom we've come to call "angels."

I put myself in that category. For my wife Patty and me, Christmas wouldn't seem complete anymore without our annual tradition of signing up through our local church to deliver gifts through Angel Tree.

We do this every year, and each family encounter is special to me. But there's one boy in particular whom I will never forget. It was ten years ago, December 1993. With packages wrapped, we headed out to the housing project where "our" family lived—a place we were warned not to visit without a police escort. We went anyway, but as we drove into the project I wondered if we'd made the right decision: We saw broken windows, trash everywhere, grim-faced gangs lounging in doorways.

When we found the apartment, a boy about nine years old cautiously opened the door. "Merry Christmas," I said, holding out the presents. "These are from your daddy."

The door swung wide open. The boy's mother was working late, and as we waited we saw that the apartment was as bleak as the courtyard outside: The furniture was torn, the stuffing falling out. A straggly Christmas tree leaned against the wall, bare of any presents.

"What's your name?" I asked the boy.

"Emmanuel," he replied.

"Emmanuel! Do you know what your name means?" I opened my Bible and read from Matthew's account of the birth of Jesus: "And they shall call him Emmanuel—which means 'God with us.'"

When the boy's mother came home, Emmanuel threw his arms around her, crying, "Mama, Mama, guess what my name means: God is with us!"

At that moment, in that clear childish voice rising above the squalor of neglected hallways and crime-filled courtyards, I heard God's good news proclaimed afresh: that he is indeed here at all times—in crime-ravaged households and with "the least of these" children.

That message comes through loud and clear in the heart-wrenching and heart-inspiring stories gathered for this book. The need is so great, but God's love—exhibited by his generous people—is so much greater.

In the history of this program, Prison Fellowship has cumulatively reached six million children. And this Christmas we hope to bring the joy of Angel Tree to more than half a million more.

I trust the stories in this book will lighten your heart—but, more, inspire you to join the host of volunteers introducing the Christ of Christmas to these needy souls.

Charles W. Colson
March 2003

*I*NTRODUCTION
WELCOMING THE CHILDREN

BY MARK L. EARLEY
PRESIDENT, PRISON FELLOWSHIP

Ty could barely sleep that night as he thought about the next day's activities. The child had written out a detailed "to do" list in his notebook: "6:00 A.M., get up; 6:05 A.M., shower; 6:10 A.M., get dressed; 6:15 A.M., eat breakfast; 6:20 A.M., wait for ride." He wasn't expecting me to pick him up until 2:00 that afternoon—almost eight hours later. But that's how excited he was! You see, I was going to drive him to a Christian summer camp.

Ty is not a prisoner's child, but he *is* a child of the inner city, a boy whose father has been absent for much of his life. I have been a mentor to Ty for several years, and during this time I have proudly watched him grow into a caring, creative, and conscientious young man. I have also seen how much his life has blessed my own.

And so, when I came to Prison Fellowship as president in early 2002, I immediately and wholeheartedly embraced the vision for Angel Tree, its ministry to prisoners' children. This is the part of our threefold focus that we refer to as "Welcoming Children," along with "Fellowshipping with Jesus" and "Visiting Prisoners."

Like Ty, these children are growing up disadvantaged by the absence of a parent and important role model in their impressionable lives. Sadly, many people on our streets are ready to exploit that void. That is why the *church* must seize the opportunity to reach out to them with unconditional love and guidance—not only to prevent them from following in their imprisoned parents' footsteps, but also, and most important, to help point them toward the Father who is *always* there for them.

The Biblical Mandate

If anyone has ever doubted that *all* children are tremendously precious to God, his own Word should put those doubts to rest. I want to focus on one particular scriptural passage—Matthew 18:1-14—and highlight some of the truths about children that God has impressed upon me.

First, **children are the measure of greatness in the divine realm** (Matthew 18:1-4). "At that time the disciples came to Jesus and asked, 'Who is the greatest in the kingdom of heaven?' He called a little child and had him stand among them. And he said: 'I tell you the truth, unless you change and become like little children, you will never enter the kingdom of heaven. Therefore, whoever humbles himself like this child is the greatest in the kingdom of heaven.'"

How often do we, like the disciples, grapple with the desire to be great? "How do I measure up to others?" we ask ourselves—examining our status, power, knowledge, ministry, and other symbols of "success."

In Jesus' day, children lacked all of those measures of importance and influence. Yet Jesus pointed to the very humility and dependency of a child as the basis—and model—for greatness in the kingdom of heaven. Children are our reminder that we must give up all claim to worldly status and treasure and depend totally on the Lord.

Second, **Jesus elevates the value of children by identifying with them** (Matthew 18:5). "Whoever welcomes a little child like this in my name welcomes me." Later, in Matthew 25, Jesus adds to the list of those with whom he shares a special relationship: the hungry, the thirsty, the stranger, the naked, the sick, the prisoner. "I tell you the truth, whatever you did for one of the least of these brothers of mine, you did for me" (Matthew 25:40).

What binds these groups together is that, in the eyes of most people, they had no practical value to society; they were marginalized, ignored, devalued. But Jesus turns that social stigma on its head. He teaches that when we serve and honor those the world pushes aside, we are actually serving and honoring *him*. And when we persist in neglecting and devaluing those on the margins, Jesus sees that as a *personal* affront. Jesus takes what is marginal and makes it central!

Third, **causing a child to sin is a dreadful offense** (Matthew 18:6). "But if anyone causes one of these little ones who believe in me to sin, it would be better for him to have a large millstone hung around his neck and to be drowned in the depths of the sea." That's very *Godfather*-esque! To look down on vulnerable children, to treat them as commodities, to cause them to stumble—such treatment receives some of Jesus' harshest words.

Fourth—and this is an extraordinary truth—**the angels of children constantly behold God's face** (Matthew 18:10). "See that you do not look down on one of these little ones. For I tell you that their angels in heaven always see the face of my Father in heaven." I'm not sure of all the implications of this statement, but one thing is clear: These angelic protectors have close proximity to the Father!

Fifth, **the Lord pays special attention to the children whom society considers most "at risk"**—those prone to stray into harm and destruction (Matthew 18:12-14). "If a man owns a hundred sheep, and one of them wanders away, will he not leave the ninety-nine on the hills and go to look for the one that wandered off? And if he finds it, I tell you the truth, he is happier about that one sheep than about the ninety-nine that did not wander off. In the same way your Father in heaven is not willing that any of these little ones should be lost."

These verses, as well as others, show the tremendous value and preciousness that Jesus bestows upon children—all children, including children of prisoners. And that is why Angel Tree is such a core part of Prison Fellowship's ministry. We take to heart God's desire that not one of these little ones should be lost or forgotten.

Society's Future

The way we treat prisoners' children—whether we welcome or shun them—can have a significant impact on the stability and security of our communities. The California-based Center for Children of Incarcerated Parents reports that the risk of prisoners' kids ending up in prison themselves is two to three times higher than the average risk. These children are also at high risk of dropping out of school, teenage pregnancy, drug abuse, and other damaging behavior. By intentionally reaching out to these children and helping redirect their paths while they are still impressionable, we are also helping to protect our community, both now and for generations to come.

Many of these children are naturally bright and talented,

but they lack the consistent caring attention and structure needed to discern and develop these gifts and use them in positive, visionary ways. With our intervention, we can give these children a genuine opportunity to grow into tomorrow's leaders, rather than tomorrow's wasted potential.

The Church's Golden Opportunity

As we read in Matthew 18:14, Jesus told his disciples, "Your Father in heaven is not willing that any of these little ones should be lost." It comes as no surprise that the humility and openness of childhood make this time of life a prime opportunity for coming to faith in Christ. In fact, the Barna Research Group has found that children aged five to thirteen have a 32-percent probability of accepting Christ as their Savior. From age fourteen through eighteen, that likelihood drops to a meager 4 percent. And for adults it barely rises to 6 percent.

Of course, we know that all things are possible with God— he can reach the hardest of hearts at whatever age. But in understanding human nature, we would be unforgivably remiss if we failed to reach out to children at a time when they are most open to trusting in Christ, before their lives and hearts are corroded by decades of sin. Like Jesus, we ought to be willing to leave our comfort zones and go out searching for these lost little ones who are so precious to him.

And, as the church, we are called not simply to share the gospel of Jesus, but also to disciple these children. In doing so, we are not just keeping them out of trouble; we are moving them *into* a life of maturity and responsibility. And we are creating a solid foundation for tomorrow's church by raising up the next generation of laborers for his kingdom.

Like Father, Like Son—and Vice Versa

I'd like to mention one more reason for the importance of welcoming children. This can become a catalyst for restoring families that have been broken apart by the ravages of crime and prison. Just as children are prone to follow in their parents' footsteps—for good or bad—so too are parents influenced by the life changes they see in their children who have been transformed by the love of Christ and his church. You will see examples of this as you read through some of the amazing stories in this book: imprisoned men and women reconciled to God and to their families because someone took the time to reach out to their children.

A Continuum of Care

Other chapters in this book will highlight the history of Angel Tree and the "nuts and bolts" of how it works. But I want to point out that what started principally as a Christmas ministry has become a *year-round* focus on ministering to prisoners' children. Currently Angel Tree Christmas is our best developed and largest program—now coordinating thousands of churches across the country to provide gifts and the gospel to more than half a million children of prisoners each December.

In addition—through Angel Tree Camping—hundreds of churches are sending prisoners' children to Christian summer camps, where they can experience well-supervised, challenging adventures; bond with caring Christian counselors; and receive exposure to biblical teaching and life applications. And with Angel Tree Mentoring, our newest program in the Angel Tree continuum, churches are being encouraged and equipped to make a significant, ongoing investment in the lives of prisoners' children by matching them with adult mentors.

I am especially committed to the growth of our mentoring program, because I know from experience the dramatic impact that loving, responsible adults can have in children's lives. As I already mentioned, for several years *I* have been a mentor to a young man named Ty. And as the former attorney general for the Commonwealth of Virginia, I helped mobilize thousands of other Virginians to come alongside young boys and girls in the same way.

In 1998, while living in Richmond, Virginia, I became a "lunch buddy" to Ty, who was then in fourth grade. I committed to meet with him at his school one Friday afternoon a month to have lunch and do homework. At the time, that was no big deal to me; I was going to eat lunch somewhere on Friday, and the school was a mere ten-minute drive from my office. But from my first meeting with Ty, I knew it was a huge deal for him. He looked up at me with an ear-to-ear smile and declared, "Mr. Earley, I am so happy to have a lunch buddy!"

Ty lived in the inner city with his mom and brother. He rarely saw his dad. His mother later told me, "I know that God sent you into our lives. Tyquon doesn't have anybody to be his father."

I have six children of my own, so pretty soon we just started including Ty in our normal family activities: taking him to the circus, inviting him over for the weekend, going to church on Sunday. Our family is loud, high-energy, and fun-loving—he fit right in! After the first weekend Ty stayed with us, he said he dreamed all the time about coming back. "I've never been in a place where it was so quiet when you lay down in bed at night and there's no gunfire."

Ty is now a teenager, and we love and accept him as part of our family. He works hard at school and wants to do well. He told me that he hopes to go to college "so that I can grow up and have a job like you have and a family like you have." He has embraced positive values I didn't intentionally set out to teach him; but as with our own children, lessons are more often caught than taught.

Someone to Guide

Unfortunately, as I learned during my four years as attorney general, many kids have never had an opportunity to "catch" the right kind of values. And instead they have succumbed to numerous counterfeit enticements that have promised to fill their empty hearts.

A few years ago, in an effort to understand and rein in youth violence in our state, I visited our youth detention facilities in Virginia and talked one-to-one with violent youthful offenders. Of all the kids I talked to, all but one had grown up without a father. Without a nurturing, caring adult relationship to guide them, they had become alienated, hostile ... and lost.

To help stop the endless repetition of this scenario, I launched a mentoring initiative that recruited four thousand volunteer mentors in Virginia by the time I left office—double the number expected! And today, as president of Prison Fellowship, I am equally passionate about enlisting and supporting positive role models to mentor the children of prisoners.

So as you read through the stories in this book, my prayer for you is that you, too, will gain a new passion for reaching out to the children of prisoners, and that you will consider ways you and your church can get involved, if you have not already done so. Remember, when you honor and welcome these children, you honor and welcome Jesus himself. And there's no greater privilege than that!

PART I

STRENGTHENING FAMILY TIES

Children of prisoners. Those two nouns define the basic eligibility criteria for participation in Prison Fellowship's Angel Tree program. But there's nothing neat and tidy about the family dynamics here. Ties have been broken. Often by the incarceration itself, but sometimes long before an arrest or guilty verdict.

Angel Tree gives imprisoned parents an opportunity to show their concern for their children, as the Christmas-season program starts when a prisoner fills out an application, asking that the gifts be given on his or her behalf.

Over the years God has orchestrated some wonderful family reunions through Angel Tree.

It was right out of *Bonnie and Clyde*. A striking, well-dressed woman, accompanied by a neatly dressed man, entered a small bank and walked up to the lone teller. At first glance, the bank teller noticed just the flaming red hair, but then he saw the shotgun in his face.

"Just give me the money, Hon," the redhead drawled.

And the teller handed it over.

Only this wasn't a movie, but the real thing. This "Bonnie" was Mary Kay Mahaffey, bank robber, safecracker. Her photo hung in the post office on the FBI "Most Wanted" list.

For five years Mary Kay ran, first with her husband, Paul, who taught her everything she needed to know about guns, safes, and bank alarms. When he ditched her, she teamed up with a couple of buddies, Joe and Ed. They pulled bank stick-ups and other thefts across the southern part of the U.S. for several years. But eventually Mary Kay's boldness and arrogance caught up.

Happily, the FBI found her before the Mafia did. In addition to eleven federal indictments, four states filed thirty-five charges against her. She was told she'd serve between 75 and 180 years.

But she didn't. Released after serving fewer than six years, she married ex-prisoner Don Beard and joined Prison Fellowship as an area director for Alabama, where she created

Angel Tree in 1982.

Today she serves as lead counselor with Impact Family Counseling and works with troubled youth in Alabama, trying to redirect youngsters away from the prison experience she and Don faced. How did she do it? How did Mary Kay Beard go from America's Most Wanted to Founder of Angel Tree?

A New Heart

Finally cornered in June 1972, Mary Kay sat in a jail cell, wondering what had become of her Christian childhood upbringing. She started attending the weekly church services held at the jail. She asked one of the volunteers why she and the others got up at 5 A.M. to minister to jail inmates. "Jesus loved all of us enough to go all the way to Calvary," the lady answered. "So we can love you enough to come here and tell you about it."

But Mary Kay was convinced that she couldn't become a Christian; her heart was too hard. Then she picked up a Bible and read, "I will give you a new heart and put a new spirit in you; I will remove from you your heart of stone and give you a heart of flesh" (Ezekiel 36:26).

The words held out a hope that she had never known. Mary Kay prayed her first prayer since childhood: "OK, God, I've made a mess of it. If you mean what you say here in Ezekiel, please change my heart."

And her life changed. A new inner peace replaced her bitterness; she stopped fighting with other inmates and asked their forgiveness. Though looking at a potential 180 years in prison, she pleaded guilty to the charges. Yet, miraculously, she was sentenced to only twenty-one years in Alabama.

Mary Kay used her time at Alabama's Julia Tutwiler Prison for Women to attend classes. She graduated from junior college with a near-perfect average and was granted a scholarship to Auburn. Four years later she completed that, with honors, and began graduate studies. She was unexpectedly paroled in 1978.

A Vision for Prisoners' Children

Now she received a new challenge. Ex-prisoner Chuck Colson, founder of Prison Fellowship, wanted her to become PF's first Alabama state director—and the first woman to serve in a PF state leadership position. She joined the staff in April 1982.

One of her first jobs was to come up with a Christmas project. Her volunteers asked which prisons they would visit and what gifts they would take. "I said, 'Everyone does that. Let's do something different.'"

Mary Kay remembered the six Christmases she had spent behind bars. "Some Christian groups would come to the prison and bring little trial-size tubes of toothpaste, bars of soap, and bottles of shampoo. I noticed that women who never went to chapel always went to those programs.

"I thought they were just greedy. I saw them bring the items back to their cells and trade with each other. [But] then they would divide the items into piles, and I realized that each pile was for one of their children. That's what they gave their children as Christmas gifts because it was all they had. And I thought, *Just because she's a thief or a drug addict, or possibly even a murderer, doesn't mean she doesn't love her children.*"

Then, during the prison's family visiting time the week

before Christmas, Mary Kay noticed as the children opened their little presents and flung their arms lovingly around their mothers. "Oh, Momma, thank you, thank you!" they squealed.

"You see," Mary Kay explains, "children don't care about things if they know they are first of all loved."

That Christmas of '82, Mary Kay went back to Tutwiler, where she had spent six years, and gathered names and addresses of the inmates' children. Then she and a handful of volunteers, with the permission of the managers, put up Christmas trees at two shopping malls, in Montgomery and Birmingham.

"We made paper angels—red for girls and green for boys—and on each angel we wrote the name and age of a child. We put them on the tree—an Angel Tree! That's how we got the name.

"I submitted an article to the newspapers about how children are victims of crime. They are not responsible for what their adult parents do, and yet they suffer. So we advertised for the public to 'come by and purchase a Christmas gift for an angel.' I hoped that we could get Christmas for two or three hundred children. I had no idea what God would do with that project."

Within six days they ran out of names and had to go back to the prison to get more. At the end of that first Angel Tree in 1982, 556 children had received up to four gifts each.

She saw another result, too—a reuniting of family ties as children received gifts from a mom or dad they had not heard from in a while.

What's more, the post-Christmas attendance at Prison Fellowship's in-prison Bible studies doubled and even tripled—bolstered by inmates whose children were Angel Tree gift recipients. "Anyone who would get my child a gift is something special," said one of the newcomers, voicing the sentiments of many. "So I decided to come and listen to this Bible study."

The program branched to twelve states the following year and was soon restructured as a church-based program. More than six hundred thousand children were reached at Christmas 2002, bringing the cumulative total to more than six million children served by Angel Tree since Mary Kay Beard first thought about those little tubes of toothpaste.

When told those numbers, Mary Kay Beard smiles. "I am both awed and humbled to have been any part of something so enormously effective. I consider it one of the highest privileges of my life. And Jesus Christ is still in the business of changing lives, I know."

"[At chapel] a lady stood up and told us that she didn't know where her children were and hadn't heard from them in some time. All she did have was a phone number, so she put that down on the Angel Tree application hoping someone could find them. She said that the volunteers were able to locate her children and deliver gifts on her behalf. Because of Angel Tree, she began receiving letters from her children and has even had a visit from them. I left the chapel in tears."

—Angel Tree volunteer

ANGEL TREE DELIVERS

1993

"Little did I know that God would use something like Angel Tree—just simple toys and simple presents—to bless my family, to turn my wife around." There's joy in the voice of ex-prisoner Jose Abreu. And gratitude. And wonder.

"It was a gift from heaven," says Jose's wife, Mayra. "That's what we thought when we received that [Angel Tree] package"—four years ago on Christmas Eve, when Mayra was living on the edge, addicted to crack cocaine.

After three years of shuffling back and forth between welfare hotels and homeless shelters, she and her three children had precariously settled in a Queens, New York, public housing apartment.

"I would go to sleep scared," says daughter Mencia, a pretty, streetwise twelve-year-old, recalling life in the shelters. "All my mother's friends were on drugs and they could come in anytime ... not even friends—strangers out of nowhere. We were scared twenty-four hours [a day]."

Mencia remembers hearing gunfire at night. "I was afraid for my mother ... that she would be dead somewhere."

Even at age seven, Mencia knew the drugs were destroying her family. "Why are you doing this, Mom? What's the matter with you?"

Mayra always had an empty answer for her daughter's pleas: "Mencia, Mencia, I'm going to stop, I promise."

The drugs had already stolen away Mencia's dad, arrested in April 1988 for two of countless burglaries to feed his hungry addiction.

Mencia tearfully recalls Jose's absence. "It's hard not to have a father ... I believed in him so much ... even when he was in prison. I loved him the same."

And even in a psychiatric institution for the criminally insane, wasted Jose found a Christian volunteer who loved him and believed in him enough to introduce him to Christ, who transformed his world.

Later in Franklin Correctional Facility, Jose attended Prison Fellowship seminars and Bible studies. With the enthusiasm of a new convert, Jose wanted to share his life-changing faith with his family—especially Mayra.

"Unfortunately, I got real pushy about it," says Jose, who showered Mayra with leaflets, tracts, Bibles. He even arranged for prison volunteers to visit Mayra and witness to her. But Mayra wanted nothing to do with Christ. And, admits Jose, "the more I pushed, the further away she got from Christianity."

Then in autumn 1989, without much thought or explanation, Jose signed up for his children to receive Christmas gifts through Angel Tree—to be purchased by PF volunteers, but delivered "from Dad."

"I filled out [the applications]," Jose remembers, "thinking it was just routine, like many other things—and many other promises."

When Jose mentioned Angel Tree to Mayra, she didn't pay much attention either, even though she hadn't bought any gifts for the children. She intended to, of course, if she could just hold on to some money....

Then on Christmas Eve, just before Mayra and the children left their apartment to spend a meager Christmas at Mayra's sister's, someone knocked on the door.

"There was a UPS guy with a BIG box," says Mayra. "We took the box into the living room and opened it. It said, 'from Jose Abreu.' Jose Abreu? How can it be? Jose's in jail. He can't buy anything!

"Then it clicked in my mind: Angel Tree!"

The kids went crazy. "It's from Daddy!" Mencia shouted. "Dad is thinking of us. Dad got us this!"

Tears well up in Mayra's eyes as she recalls, "My kids were crying and jumping up and down and hugging me, 'Mommy! Look what I have!'"

A doll for Mencia. A space shuttle for Alejandro. A farm for Enriquillo. Clothes for everyone.

"That is when I cried out to God, and I knew that he loved me," says Mayra. "I accepted the Lord Jesus Christ into my life.

"And then I prayed with my kids," Mayra continues. "I said, 'God, please help me to stop this bad habit I have ... I don't want it anymore.... Take this drug addiction away from me please so I can be a responsible parent ... the mom they deserve to have.'"

At that moment, Jesus delivered Mayra from her addiction. The Abreu family was free at last. It was a gift from heaven.

"When Mom accepted Christ, I was right there," says Mencia. "And I accepted Christ with her.

"It's a total change for our family—reuniting, getting to know what love is all about."

And Jose was part of that reuniting, coming home to his family in July 1990. "I didn't walk out of prison by myself," Jose proclaims. "I brought Jesus with me."

"We [started doing] fun things together that we had never done before," says Mayra. "We went to the beach, the park, the museum of natural history, movies, the amusement park, and camping every summer." And, to the children's great relief, there were "no more addict friends coming around, no more drug dealers knocking on the door, no more hiding, no more lying."

To this day, they do not know the identity of the PF volunteer or volunteers who sent that UPS package on Jose's behalf. Whoever you are, Jose and Mayra—and Mencia and her brothers—say thank you. To them, you are a gift from heaven.

Postscript 2003

Ever since the day that UPS package arrived more than a decade ago, Jose and Mayra Abreu bear witness to the life-saving power of Jesus Christ. In fact, they're both in the life-saving business now.

They both enlisted in prison ministry through Prison Fellowship. Jose conducts PF seminars—including *Free at Last,* which addresses drug addiction. For four years he directed Door to Life Ministry, a church-based, residential drug-treatment center.

Mayra works part-time in the New York City PF office, heavily immersed in Angel Tree logistics. Mencia, too, has been a regular participant in Angel Tree: All four years in her *public* high school she recruited students to help purchase gifts—hanging the paper angel ornaments on school bulletin boards so classmates could choose specific prisoners' children.

And ten years ago, the Abreus moved into a much more personalized children's ministry when they began to welcome prisoners' infants into their family.

Mayra and other volunteers regularly visited the female inmates at Rikers Island—including the nursery, where qualifying mothers who bore children while in prison could keep the newborns with them for one year. Then one day a mother asked, "What will you do for my *child?*"

That's when Jose and Mayra started making arrangements with concerned mothers and Family Court to receive legal custody of the children and care for them like their own—until the mom was released and the court deemed her stable enough to reclaim her child.

Since then, ten children have come through the Abreu household—boys and girls, some short-term, some indefinitely. Right now their extended family includes Isaac, ten, whom they have cared for since he was born; Kevin, eight, who also came to them as an infant; and Kevin's baby brother Kiano, a year old.

Thankfully, they now have more room for this ever-expanding family. Last summer the Abreus moved into their new four-bedroom house in Queens, a once-rundown mess strikingly overhauled by Habitat for Humanity volunteers. The Abreus put in a collective six hundred hours of manual labor, the equivalent of a down payment. For the first time, they have a fenced-in yard where the children can safely play.

"I love these kids so much," says Mayra, speaking of all the prisoners' children who have come and are yet to come. "When I first see them, they are so little, so defenseless, so vulnerable. They don't have anyone else to be there for them."

Meanwhile, God's care and strength have kept Jose and Mayra going through some difficult times. On April 18, 2000, both went under the surgeon's knife, when part of Mayra's healthy liver was transplanted into Jose, replacing an organ irreversibly destroyed by decades of drug and alcohol binges. She saved his life.

While Jose could take no post-operative painkillers because they might trigger liver rejection, Mayra could take no painkillers because any hint of a narcotic now makes her horribly nauseous. "When the Lord delivered me from drugs, he delivered me completely!" she proclaims.

But even after the post-surgical pain wore off, Jose faced a long and rutted recovery—over two years of repeated trips to the hospital for blood infections; blood clots; symptoms of liver rejection; misadjusted medications that set off hallucinations, acute depression, even psychosis. Yet in the struggle, "I saw the power of God in my life," he says. "God never left me alone." In August 2002 physicians finally gave him a "thumbs up" to seek employment again.

Another cloud has hovered over the family the last two years: Jose, who has kept his green-card status in the U.S., faces the threat of deportation for his past acts of "moral turpitude." Chuck Colson and other Prison Fellowship leaders have rallied to his defense; his lawyer's court documents detail the evidences of a truly transformed life. So far, his legal hearing has been postponed.

"But God is the One who takes care of me," says Jose with confidence. "I rely on the Lord."

"My husband and I have known of your wonderful ministry for years.... We had prayed about how to have our children get a heart for GIVING this Christmas. We heard the Steven Curtis Chapman Angel Tree CD with the testimony of an entire family saved through Angel Tree. Each of our three children got to choose a ministry that they could give $50 to. When they heard the testimony of the Abreu family, Emily, our seven-year-old, wanted to give to Angel Tree, so here we are, better late than never. Your work is eternal and keep it up and let no seed of the enemy take root."

—*Angel Tree contributor*

"*If* It Weren't for Angel Tree..."

2000

Jenny Phillips* hung up the phone in disbelief. She had recognized Elizabethann Francis' name when she got the phone message; she had been attending Elizabethann's tiny church, Camino Real Community Church in Boca Raton, Florida, for a few months. When Jenny returned the call, Elizabethann asked what her children wanted for Christmas. Jenny's estranged husband Andrew had signed them up for Angel Tree, and now Jenny's own church wanted to provide the gifts.

But Jenny had left Andrew in a West Coast prison. She hadn't told him where she and the children were going—or even that they were leaving. How had Angel Tree found them? And how did his application happen to wind up in her own church?

Elizabethann was baffled, too. Finding Jenny's children on her Angel Tree list had startled her. Until then, she says, "no one had ever said a word about Jenny being alone or her husband in jail." But she realized one thing—God was doing something; she just was not sure exactly what. "We need to pray about this," she told Jenny.

Jenny, however, was in no hurry to renew contact with Andrew. She'd had enough.

An abusive youthful marriage had ended in divorce. Another relationship produced two children, but little love.

* *The family's name has been changed at their request.*

Then Andrew, her new husband and the father of her infant daughter, also took his anger out on her, first verbally. He agreed to get counseling, but when he hit her—just once—he crossed a line. For Jenny, there was no going back.

She pressed charges, and while Andrew sat in prison, Jenny's father flew out West, packed up the family, and moved Jenny and her three children to Boca Raton. "I didn't tell Andrew. I didn't talk to him, nothing," she admits. "I didn't want to have anything to do with him again."

Starting a new life, Jenny tried to get her priorities straight. "I said the first thing I have to do is find a church."

During her childhood, Jenny's parents had taken her to church "every Sunday without fail," she says. "I couldn't stand church when I was little. It was really boring to me, and I was always in trouble."

Jenny partied through high school until a coworker at a grocery store took her to his church. "I got saved. At first you're on a high like when you get a present or a new friend. It was like that for about a year." But without family support Jenny lost her fervor and spiritual interest and rarely went to church.

Andrew's mother took him to church sporadically during an abusive childhood. But he and Jenny both realized God was missing from their lives. "We always said, 'We need to go to church,'" she recalls. But "every time we meant to go, something happened—the car broke down, or it just never worked out."

So when she and her children arrived in Florida in May 1999, she enlisted her parents and a cousin in a search for a church. But at one affluent church after another, "the people weren't very friendly," Jenny recalls. "We got really discouraged. So finally I told my mom, 'I'm done. I'm not looking for a church anymore. We will just pray at home.'" But her mother believed the family needed a church and refused to accept defeat. "Let me try one more time," she said. So she ventured out one more Sunday and found Camino Real Community Church.

"You're gonna love it," she promised Jenny. "It's small. Everybody is really, really nice. Let's just try." So she persuaded Jenny to load up the children and visit Camino Real. "When I first went to Camino Real, I was just relieved to have people smile at me and be kind to my kids," Jenny says. And Jenny kept going back.

"I used to sit in the back of the church by myself and write letters to an old friend. My letters got shorter and shorter until I couldn't stop listening to Pastor David; he is so honest. I specifically remember him saying, 'I left home in a cop car at seventeen,' and that hit home for me; I had been running since I was like fifteen years old. I never knew what I was looking for until I sat in that church and really listened, and I realized I wanted unconditional love because I never had it before. But if I would have just stopped and listened, I would have realized I always had it from God."

That October Elizabethann Francis set the stage for the church's Angel Tree project, recruiting volunteers to buy gifts and organize a Christmas party for prisoners' families. When the Prison Fellowship area office sent her a list of Angel Tree kids in Boca Raton, Elizabethann contacted the families, including Jenny.

"I said, 'You've got to be kidding!'" Jenny recalls. "Andrew was in prison on the West Coast, and he sent our name in to Angel Tree, not really knowing for sure where we were. And they happened to find us. I thought, *This can't be real. How could this happen?* I mean this church is so small"—fewer than eighty adults. Jenny agreed to take the children to the church's Angel Tree Christmas brunch.

"We went to the party, and there were stacks of presents for each one of my kids. Stacks!" As her children ecstatically tore into their gifts, "I totally broke down," she says, breaking down again as she remembers. "I went into the church by myself after they opened their presents, and I prayed about it. Then I finally wrote to Andrew.

"When I first wrote Andrew, I said a lot of things that weren't nice because I was still so angry and hurt and resentful," she confesses.

Writing back, Andrew told Jenny what his life had been like in prison. He'd suffered a stroke, and the physical vulnerability coupled with the loss of his family had jolted him emotionally: *Maybe I'm not really in charge.* The new realization had prompted him to sign up for anger-management classes and attend chapel; he'd prayed and given his life to Christ. Subsequently another inmate had attacked him with a razor, but—he knew this would be hard for Jenny to believe—he had not responded with anger. When Angel Tree applications were distributed to the inmates, Andrew took a gamble. He knew Jenny had relatives in Florida, so he filled out the application to be sent simply to Boca Raton. Now, he assured her, he had changed. "Let's give it another chance," he pleaded.

Jenny wasn't so sure. When Andrew was released, he stayed with friends and got a temporary job as he tried to persuade

Jenny to let him rejoin the family. He called on their little girl's birthday. "We both sobbed on the phone and said a lot of [previously] unsaid things: things that bothered us, things we missed about each other, things we didn't miss, how badly he missed me and the kids, and his chances of coming here," Jenny says.

He saved his money, hoping Jenny would eventually tell him to come to Florida. He bought calling cards to stay in contact. Jenny finally told him, "OK, if you really want to come, this is my pastor's phone number. You need to call him and talk to him first, and then we'll take it from there."

Andrew hung up the phone and immediately dialed Pastor David Seabrooke, who asked to see Andrew the very day he came to Boca Raton.

The children were already asleep the night Andrew arrived; Jenny stayed up to wait for him. "He came into my room, and I jumped up off the bed straight into his arms. Then I cried. I love Andrew with all my heart and always have; I just knew it would be OK the second I saw him—his whole face had just changed." On Sunday he attended church with the family, and after the service met with Pastor Seabrooke. They started counseling right away.

At the church's men's Bible study, Andrew took a bold step and confessed his past behavior toward Jenny. There he made friends who mentor him as he grows in his faith—this summer the group focused on being the men God wants them to be. One of the church's elders is leading Andrew through a discipleship program. Jenny, who is studying for child-care certification, helps out with several of the church's ministries. And the children are active in Sunday school.

One day last spring, the children cornered Elizabethann. "They stopped to tell me 'thank you,'" she says. "I asked 'why?' They said their stepfather—Andrew—was a changed man, and they knew he loved their mother and loved them." This past July, Andrew and Jenny were baptized.

"It's unbelievable," Jenny insists. "He's changed totally. It's not like we don't argue, because we do. But there's no fighting.

"But if it weren't for Angel Tree, I would never have written to him," Jenny says. "I would never have thought that it was a sign from God or that he was ready to change. I would have just let it all go."

GET THE PICTURE?

1996

To get gift ideas for a prisoner's sixteen-year-old son, Dorcas Wilkinson telephoned the boy's grandmother-guardian. The grandmother seemed "elusive—like she wasn't crazy about talking about her daughter in prison," says Wilkinson, Angel Tree coordinator for El Paso, Texas. So Wilkinson asked if she could talk to the boy.

When he came to the phone, Wilkinson introduced herself and asked if there was something she could get him for Christmas—on behalf of his mother. "I don't need anything, Mrs. Wilkinson," the teen answered politely. But when pressed he added, "Well, there is something I want very much."

"I saw visions of Cadillacs in my mind," says Wilkinson. But all the boy asked for was a picture of his mother—whom he hadn't seen for almost three years. Not a single photo of her adorned his grandmother's house.

Unsure of the prison's policies, Wilkinson said she would try her best. She immediately wrote to one of the chaplains, explained the son's Christmas request, and asked if a photograph could be taken. The chaplain called back with good news: The warden had granted special permission.

One glitch: The inmate had to pay for the photo—about four dollars, which she couldn't afford. Wilkinson provided the money and received the photo, which she framed.

"Thank you for the gifts you gave my children this year. It has been sixteen months since my daughter last wanted to talk to me. But when she got the Angel Tree presents from me, she wanted to talk to me right away and will visit me soon. Thank you, Jesus."

—*Prisoner-Dad*

$\mathscr{A}$ Dad for Sage

2002

Baby Sage was almost never born. After a three-month fling, his mother, Angela, had gotten pregnant. A single mom already, she felt she just couldn't afford to care for another child on her own. She set an appointment at the local abortion clinic, waiting up until Maine's legal limit of sixteen weeks to make her decision.

But as Angela gathered her things to go to the clinic, Sage gave a great kick. Angela broke down. She knew this baby was alive ... and that she could never have him aborted. She missed her appointment—and delivered a healthy baby boy on April 8, 1997.

Sage's dad never even knew he existed until Sage was already three years old. He heard it through mutual friends, but never visited, and never paid child support—even though he lived in the same town as his son.

Every weekend, when Angela's older son Garrett's father took his son out, little Sage became very sad. "I want a dad," he would say. "I need my dad. Mommy, can you get married so I can have a dad, too?"

There seemed to be little hope that Sage's dad would ever have a role in his life. But then, Sage's father was sentenced to spend a year in the Maine State Correctional Facility. And something inside of him changed forever.

When Angela heard that her child's father had signed up

to participate in the Angel Tree program, she was shocked. "I never heard of Angel Tree before," she says. "This lady called me for weeks ... and I blew her off. I didn't want any ties with the father."

But that Christmas, Maine experienced its worst winter in years, with subzero temperatures. On welfare and drowning in financial troubles, Angela grudgingly accepted the woman's offer. "Two people showed up at our house, their arms loaded with gifts," Angela says. "I told Sage and my older son, Garrett, that they were from Santa."

Out from the boxes came thick warm coats, food, snowsuits, jackets, boots, socks, jeans, shirts, Bibles, books. "I was so thrilled," Angela gushes. "I just couldn't believe it! At first I was angry that his deadbeat father would try to mess with my son's head. But now, I am so thankful!"

When Sage's father got out of prison, he contacted his son. "I'm warning you," Angela told him bluntly. "You had better be consistent, or don't even bother." On Sage's fifth birthday, he and his father met for the first time—over dinner at his dad's apartment.

"He's like a new kid!" Angela exclaims. "And his father is amazing! He's been out for a year and a half now, and he takes Sage out every other weekend. They go to the gym together, they go ice-fishing together, and they spend a lot of time out-doors.

"At first when his father came into Sage's life, he spoiled him. I think prison made him realize how precious life really was. Sage would come home every night with a huge banana split! But now, they are starting to have a normal relationship. The father is even paying child support!"

Sage's dad is keeping down a good job, too, finding consistent work for the first time in his life. And Angela is taking classes at the University of Maine, studying to get her degree in mental health and human services. "I want to be a social worker," she says. "I know just what it feels like to be caught in the system."

Sage is struggling a little in school, but now he has his dad as a role model. "His father goes in and talks to Sage's teachers," Angela says. "I never imagined he would be this involved in Sage's life. It is wonderful!"

And Sage and Garrett now attend a Christian day-care center at the Open Door Church, right across the street from their home. "It is so great to know that they are in a safe place while I am away," Angela says. "God is truly looking out for these boys. It's been hard, but after Angel Tree things have been so different. I could not imagine my life without them."

A Family Says Yes to a Father

1994

Boyd, a prisoner in Florida, hadn't spoken to his ex-wife, Sonja, or nine-year-old son, Drew, for almost three years. "I was a poor father and had a habit of 'selling dreams' to her and my son," he wrote in a letter to PF staff. "She got tired and cut me off."

Although Boyd had repeatedly tried to contact them, Sonja refused to accept his phone calls or answer his letters, even after Boyd had written of becoming "a new man" in Jesus Christ.

"I knew I had done so much damage in the past that it would be hard for her to believe," he admitted. But Boyd prayed that she would forgive him—and allow him a second chance to be a father. Then, this past fall, he signed up for Drew to receive Angel Tree gifts.

But Boyd got his own surprise gift when he phoned his dad the day after Christmas. Sonja had sent a message: Tell Boyd to call; this time she would accept the charges!

When he got through, Sonja chatted about the gifts the volunteers had delivered: a sweater, a basketball, a tie "to wear to church," a children's Bible with Drew's name engraved on it. But Sonja's next words "blew me away!" said Boyd. Drew wanted to see him, so would he please add their names to the prison visiting list? She planned to bring him soon—all the way from Ohio to Florida.

Then she handed the phone to Drew, and with his heart pummeling his chest, the repentant father asked for—and received—his son's forgiveness. "I love you, Dad"—those priceless, longed-for words. "I think about you every day."

"God *over*-answered my prayers!" Boyd wrote to PF. "I don't know if you receive many thank-you letters, but I just had to let you know that God is using your ministry.... God bless you all."

CARLY GOES TO CAMP

2000

Carly Fanti is a sweet thirteen-year-old girl whose father has been in prison ever since she was born. When Carly was small, she didn't know where her dad was; she only knew she received a Christmas gift from him every year through Angel Tree.

But when she was seven, her mom told her the whole story. Even at such a young age, Carly was devastated. Angry and bitter, she had a hard time trusting anyone, especially God. Even though Carly went to church with her mom, it seemed like God wasn't really there. How could God love her and yet leave her without a father?

For four months Carly told no one about her family's secret. It was too embarrassing. She felt so alone. But God was there. That summer a Prison Fellowship volunteer named Howard Waller arranged for Carly to go to Camp Redcloud, a week-long camp just for Angel Tree kids.

Camp opened up a whole new world for Carly. "I saw there were other kids who are going through the same thing," she says. "I realized I was not the only one and that I shouldn't feel sorry for myself."

More important, Carly realized that her heavenly Father was there and that he loved her. She accepted Christ as her Savior, and she hasn't been the same since.

As fun as it was to go horseback riding, rappelling, hiking, and canoeing, it wasn't these things that stuck with her it was a simple camp song she learned:

Father, I adore you; lay my life before you; how I love you ...

When Carly got back, her mom, Lori, could really see the difference. "She wouldn't stop singing that song!" Lori says. "She just ran around the house singing it over and over again."

One year later, Carly had the chance to proclaim the change in her life at an Angel Tree banquet at the Governor's Mansion in Denver. In front of five hundred people, she shyly told her story and sang the song she had learned at camp: *"Father, I adore You ..."*

There wasn't a dry eye in the place.

Camp changed Carly's father, Dennis, too. Carly and Lori became a tag-team force, encouraging him to attend PF seminars and Bible studies in prison. And as his relationship with Christ deepened, he was finally able to understand God's forgiveness. "Because of your love, and your faith in Christ, my life has changed," he told his wife and daughter.

But seeking Carly's forgiveness seemed a lot tougher. "Not too long ago, I got really angry with my dad," Carly said openly. "We wrote and talked on the phone and stuff, but I didn't want to write him anymore. I was angry that he wasn't there to see me play volleyball or run track, and that he wasn't there to see me in the choir."

On one of her visits to prison, Lori explained the situation to her husband. The next week Carly received a four-page letter from her father. In it, Dennis apologized for hurting her and for the shame and embarrassment he had caused.

It was the first time he had ever owned up to the pain he

had caused without blaming his own abusive childhood or drugs. "Prison isn't my punishment," he wrote. "My punishment is not being able to watch you grow up."

Carly has been to camp several times now, working hard to earn the money to go by selling candy bars and raising scholarship money from families in her church, Holy Cross Lutheran. But she hasn't been able to go for the past two years, and she really misses it.

Lori says, "Camp meets the needs of these kids in two important ways. First, they get to go somewhere they would never be able to go normally. Many children are being raised by grandparents and single parents, and we just don't have the money.

"Second, they get to talk with kids that are going through the same thing. No more secrets, no more heavy burdens. Even if some of them already know Jesus, and most do not, camp is a time for their spirits to be refilled, refreshed, and renewed."

Dear Angel Tree:
Thank you—God used your gifts to bring happiness and joy to many children and their families during the Christmas holiday. We had the incredible joy of meeting and visiting with each of the families as their gifts were delivered. But there is one family in particular that I'd like you to meet.

This is a Hispanic family with three children ranging in ages from five to eleven. The youngest is a little girl who cries herself to sleep each night. She is sad because she thinks her father doesn't love her because he doesn't come home to her. I picked them up to bring them to the open house [at which Angel Tree gifts were presented].

As we visited in the car, I asked if they understood why we were giving them gifts. Then I explained that it was because their father loved them and wanted them to have something from him for Christmas but wasn't able to purchase them himself. Therefore, he had asked that we do this for him. I was curious as to the silent response to this explanation, and upon peering into the rearview mirror, I saw that all three children had tears streaming down their faces.

When they arrived at the open house, we gave them a tour. Donald Stanley made them each a balloon animal, which they said was the best part of the program. Their tummies were filled with food, which we found out was their breakfast. After they ate, we took them to the Christmas tree, nativity scene, and manger. There Daniel England, dressed as Joseph, and Nicole Sarver, dressed as Mary, told this little family the Christmas story.

We explained that God loved them and sent Jesus so that they could have eternal life and a heart filled with peace. All four of them responded to the gospel and asked Jesus into their hearts. That day, they left with happy hearts, a bag of gifts, and the greatest gift of all, Jesus.

A few days later, the mom called to say thank you for the gifts and the party. She was really excited. You see, we had found out that the children call their father Popi and had signed their gift tags with his name. When the children saw that they were from "Popi," they became excited. Finally, they all know that their father really does love them.

—*Angel Tree volunteer*

$\mathcal{F}$ATHER AND CHILD REUNION

2000

Raquel Medina remembers decorating plates for Mother's and Father's Day gifts. As the grammar-school teacher handed out the plates—two to each child—a classmate spoke up.

"Raquel doesn't need two. She doesn't have a dad."

"Yes I do," Raquel snapped back.

"Yes, Raquel does have a dad," her teacher agreed, and gave her two plates to work on. But Raquel doesn't remember ever giving her dad his plate. And she couldn't bring herself to admit to the other kids that he was, well, in prison.

Ernest Medina first went to prison when Raquel was ten. He seemed to seek out trouble, dealing drugs, jumping bail, driving without a license. More often than not he lived behind locked doors. Occasionally he came home to Colorado Springs. *Maybe he'll stay this time,* she would think. But no. Soon he was gone again.

Eager to stabilize her family life, Raquel's mother took her three daughters to church. As a child, Raquel accepted Christ as her Savior. "My mom made sure I had spiritual mentors," she says—adults who prayed with and for her, who discipled and encouraged her. Her mom also assured her that God was her Father: "a Father to the fatherless." And throughout adolescence, Raquel talked to God as if he were her dad, asking him to take care of her.

When Raquel was fourteen or fifteen, her two fathers—the one in heaven and the one in prison—teamed up with Prison Fellowship Angel Tree volunteers for two years to provide Christmas gifts for Raquel and her younger sisters, Monique and Danielle.

Accustomed to wearing secondhand clothes, Raquel welcomed the new coats and the other gifts—including a Bible with her name on it—the Angel Tree volunteers brought. But she'd become so self-reliant, she resented the help. "I didn't think I needed anyone," she says. "I was excited to get the presents, but I didn't want to *need* them."

And later in high school she decided she didn't need her father either. "I quit praying for him."

In August 1995 Raquel flew east to enroll at Trinity International University, a Christian school near Chicago. She made new friends and buried herself in the books. For two years she heard nothing from Ernest, though during her sophomore year, he crept back into her prayer life. "God burdened my heart for him," she remembers, preparing her for the phone call that would beckon her back into his life.

She was home for summer break in late July 1997 when a local newscast claimed Raquel's dad had been shot—critically—by police. He'd skipped bail—again. Under Colorado's "three strikes" law, this meant he was up for sixteen years in prison. Unwilling to face that kind of time, he baited the officers who came to arrest him, pretending he had a weapon. So they shot him. Four times.

Doctors didn't expect Ernest to live; neither did he. Thinking this might be their last chance to see him, Raquel and her sisters went to visit him, once, then twice. "He was angry with everyone," she recalls. Raquel tried to talk to him, but "he just didn't want to hear about God," she says.

In fact, he didn't really want to see anyone, Raquel remembers. "He yelled at Danielle, so she just started to walk out. Then he yelled, 'Come back here.' But then he'd say, 'I don't want to see you.'"

Sad and discouraged, Raquel flew back to Trinity for the new school year. "I didn't understand why he didn't turn to God," she says. Nonetheless, "God began to soften my heart for my dad." His life had been spared. Wasn't there a reason?

Raquel returned to Colorado Springs for the holidays, in time to see Danielle in the Christmas play at Woodman Valley Chapel. Still recovering, Ernest got permission to attend one performance, and Raquel purposely stayed home that night.

But Danielle called Raquel from the church. "Raquel, Daddy has changed," she insisted. "He's really different."

Remembering the anger in his face at the hospital, and his indifference to the Lord, Raquel needed proof that he had changed. The next day he called Raquel to chat. And she was convinced. "It wasn't anything he said," she recalls. "It was that he was concerned about *me* rather than talking about himself. He was genuinely interested in *me!*"

She learned that his narrow escape from death had ultimately brought Ernest Medina to Christ. "He thought, *God must really want me here for a reason,*" Raquel says. And he knew she'd been praying for him.

Ernest was sent back to prison in June 2000. Raquel was able to spend one day with him before his incarceration, starting to build the relationship they'd never had. Now they call and write each other regularly. "It's amazing; it's what I've longed for all my life," Raquel says. Seeing evidence of change in his life, she says, "it was easy to forgive him" for past hurts.

In his Colorado prison, Ernest became active in Prison Fellowship Bible studies. He no longer seeks out trouble. He now seeks out new prisoners, to tell them about Bible studies, shop class, and support groups, hoping to shield them from some of the worst aspects of prison life. "And he's taken that initiative himself!" Raquel boasts.

"When I am down or discouraged, all I have to do is think about my dad," she says. And she talks about him—no longer with embarrassment but with pride. "I love telling people about my dad." His transformation. His witness. His faithful God. "God didn't give up on my dad even when I did!"

Postscript 2003

Raquel still lives in the Chicago area, now married and a mother of two. She received a bachelor's degree in youth ministry with a minor in biblical studies from Trinity International University in Deerfield, Illinois. During a college summer, she counseled four girls at Boys' Town in Omaha, Nebraska. After graduation, she returned to Trinity as a residence director and assistant activities director. "I want to build relationships with youth and be a support to them," she explains. She wants to live out the love she and Ernest have received from their heavenly Father—and his church.

"I feel that I will always be involved with youth. Currently, I have the privilege of investing in college-age women who are in different stages of their lives. These are informal times over a meal or just getting together."

Her dad's remarkable recovery from the shootings continues.

While at the Colorado Territorial Correctional Facility, he underwent multiple surgeries and other medical treatment to enable him to use his left hand and right arm. Raquel stays in touch with him through monthly phone calls and letters. "My dad is continuing to grow in his relationship with the Lord, but like any person, there are times when he struggles. He does have a group of godly men in his life who challenge and encourage him."

Ernest developed a close relationship with Chaplain Dan Canady (a former Prison Fellowship area director) and served as a chapel clerk. Ernest also served as the inside team leader for the prison's Kairos program. Chaplain Canady represented Ernest at Raquel's wedding.

Ernest has since been transferred to a low-security facility to complete his sentence. He appreciates the miraculous nature of his continuing reconciliation with Raquel: "For God to have taken us as far as he has, I couldn't ask for more."

Ernest also praises his wife, Pat: "If it hadn't been for her strength in God, it would have been a lot rougher for me." He shared Raquel's concern that he has some ways to go with her sisters: "But we have come a long way from where we were."

$\mathcal{B}$ack From the Brink

1996

Anaheim First Christian Church in Southern California serves a neighborhood on the edge: on the edge of gang activity and drug dealing and violence, on the edge of poverty and despair. In July 1994 Jodi Armstrong and her teenaged son, Andrew, rented a small apartment across the alley behind the church. They were the remnants of a family living on the edge—touched by drugs, violence, and poverty. Jodi's husband, Bob, was in prison. Her two younger children were someplace—she wasn't sure where—in the foster-care system. At age fifteen Andrew had a police record of his own and a ready anger. And now he was casing the neighborhood gangs, looking for a place to belong, a fight to pick.

Fortunately he also checked out the basketball court at First Christian, and there he made friends who drew him into church activities. Soon Andrew was nudging Jodi to join him at WOW—Worship On Wednesdays. The program started with dinner, all you could eat for two dollars, followed by singing, worship, and classes. Afterward a group lingered in the church parking lot, watching the nightly array of fireworks falling like star dust over nearby Disneyland.

Angel Work

At First Christian, Jodi didn't hide the fact that her husband was in prison, that her life was in shambles. It was hard for church members not to flinch at the vulgarities that punctuated her every paragraph. But Pastor Bob Kuest didn't wring his hands or scold or turn his back. He pointed her to Harbor House, the church annex that houses neighborhood-outreach ministries. And there Jodi found Prison Fellowship volunteers Neal and Judy Odom. Open hearts. Listening ears. Busy workers. Role models who live out their faith.

Jodi wondered if the church could help her—specifically by finding and paying for transportation to visit Bob in prison, at the other end of the state. Being an ex-prisoner himself, Neal understood the problem, and he started to work on solutions. But he didn't leave it at that. He explained Prison Fellowship's vision for reaching out to prisoners' families through Angel Tree—volunteers buying and delivering Christmas gifts for prisoners' children. Gifts given on behalf of the parent in prison—to help maintain family ties, to alleviate hardship, and to demonstrate the love of Christ and the church.

Even though Christmas was months away, evidence of Angel Tree was stacking up at Harbor House—a clearinghouse for Angel Tree in Southern California. Toy trucks. Dolls. Boxed clothing. Basketballs. Donations destined for homes like Jodi's, for children like Andrew. The vision and the volunteers drew Jodi in. Soon she was knocking on the door, asking if she could help sort gifts, wrap packages.

One day Jodi wistfully mentioned her two younger children. Did Neal think Angel Tree could reach them—even though they were "lost" to the family?

Neal took a deep breath and accepted the challenge. "Give me the social worker's name, and I'll see if there's anything we can do." Maybe his letter was delivered by an angel, because permission was granted. Angel Tree could contact the children and provide gifts in Bob's name.

And that special delivery broke open Jodi's hardened heart. She came to church on Sunday mornings. She wanted to stick with this church and these people. She'd been keeping watch, and she was seeing more than fizzling fireworks.

Heart Work

In January the church paid Andrew's way to go to a Christian camp up in the mountains. The next Sunday, back in Anaheim, he told the whole congregation that he'd committed his life to Jesus. Then and there the youth minister lowered Andrew into the waters of baptism: buried with Christ, raised to a new life.

In February Jodi accepted Christ as Savior and Lord. She was clear about her decision, but she asked for an exception to the church's pattern of immediate baptism. She wanted to wait and be baptized after Bob got out of prison. For several months Neal had been writing Bob, encouraging him to give God room to work in his life. Neal had sent Bob some basic Prison Fellowship Bible study booklets and pointed him to Bible study groups led by PF volunteers.

In March Bob was paroled. Bob's first Sunday back home, Neal and Judy and their son, Neal, Jr., who had befriended Andrew from the start, took the family out to lunch after church. Over the next few weeks Bob noticed the marked difference in his family: language cleaner, drugs dropped, anger abated. Something was going on here that he wanted to be part of.

Several weeks later as Easter was approaching, the pastor called Jodi's name for baptism. She stood and, to her amazement, so did Bob. "I'm coming with you," he said. "I'm ready to commit my life to Christ, too."

That Sunday in May 1996 the angels in heaven rejoiced as a husband and wife joined their hearts to the heart of God. The fireworks in heaven weren't coming from Disneyland.

Family Work

The Armstrong family still had a lot of work ahead of them. They've been willing to face tough issues in individual and family counseling. They're learning to set up and hold to a family budget. They're working with the social service agency to meet requirements that would allow them to regain custody of their younger children.

And their church family is pulling for them: replacing furniture lost in an unfortunate fire, paying for temporary housing. Early in October the church gave Bob a scholarship to attend a Prison Fellowship conference for Christian ex-prisoners.

Back in Anaheim, you might well find Bob and Jodi and Andrew tending the grounds of First Christian: their contribution to thank the church family for helping them draw back from life on the edge.

Postscript 2003

Today, the Armstrong family is intact, and still a part of Anaheim First Christian Church. This past Christmas, Andrew joined his parents in delivering gifts to other Angel Tree children.

One day, a grandmother who cares for an eight-year-old girl whose father is in prison received a telephone call from an Angel Tree volunteer. The volunteer asked what the child would like for Christmas.

"A doll," the volunteer heard the little girl answer her grandmother in the background.

"The doll is coming from your daddy," the grandmother said. "What kind do you want?"

The child said, "So long as it's from my daddy, any kind of doll will do."

PART II

Working from information given by the prisoner, a volunteer usually calls the child's caregiver (parent or guardian) to ask what the child needs or wants for Christmas, one clothing item and one toy. Then gift delivery is arranged—either at the home or at a church-sponsored event or party.

For many volunteers or prisoners' families, gift delivery has been a memorable experience of grace: Logistical problems are resolved. Needs known only to God are suddenly met. The Good News is explained. The right word is spoken at the right moment. The spirit of Christmas graces the generosity of God's people.

$\mathcal{B}$RAILLE BIBLE BEATS OUT BARBIE

2002

Angel Tree volunteer John Miller was calling children's care-givers for gift suggestions when he reached the mother of Tiffany, a fourteen-year-old. He noted from the application that her incarcerated father had asked for headphones, tennis shoes, and books for Tiffany. John asked Tiffany's mother what kind of books the girl would like.

"Sir, my daughter is blind," said the mother. "She has been blind since birth."

But John was undaunted.

"How about books in Braille?" he asked. "Does she read Braille?"

"Yes, but books in Braille are expensive and hard to find," said the mom. "Do you think it would be possible?"

"Madam," assured the former marine, "nothing is impossible."

On the gift tag for Angel 260A, John wrote, "Books in Braille." Then he hung it along with the other tags on the Angel Tree at Community Baptist Church in Manhattan Beach, California.

Following church services the next Sunday, sisters Amanda and Evelyn Kenney went up to the Angel Tree to choose their tree tags. Their father, Sean, steered eight-year-old Evelyn to the tags for twin girls her own age, who asked for Barbie dolls and clothing. Those would be easy items to find, he reasoned. Instead, Evelyn focused her attention on Tag 260A and asked her father what "Braille" meant.

"It means she is probably blind," said Sean, wondering where one would start looking for a book in Braille. Again he tried to interest Evelyn in the tags for the twins, but Evelyn removed Tiffany's tag and insisted, "This is the one."

Sean and his wife, Rosangela, went to work. "We found some bookstores on the Internet and called them," says Sean. "While they would sell books through the mail, we weren't sure about the titles, and none of them could deliver by Christmas. So we contacted the Braille Institute in Los Angeles."

They spoke with George, who told them about book programs for young people. The Institute kept some Braille books in stock, he explained, and had a bookstore on site.

"We decided that we should see them that same afternoon," Sean recalls, "so my wife brought Evelyn and Amanda to my work after school, and by 3:30 the three of us were on our way. It was a fifty-mile ride."

Surprised that they had shown up so quickly, George asked what Tiffany liked to read. "We had to explain that we didn't know the girl," says Sean, and that required some additional explanation. "So we shared with George the Angel Tree ministry, how men and women in prison work through chaplains and local churches to arrange for gifts to be given to [prisoners'] children so that they can have a Christmas."

George then told the Kenneys that he had heard about a Bible arriving recently, a copy of the King James Version in Braille.

"We said we would be very interested in getting a Bible for Tiffany."

George then called his supervisor, who listened carefully as Sean explained why they wanted to buy a Bible for a blind girl they had never met.

But the Bible they had just received was not for sale, she said. It would be given free in trust. Inside were instructions to return the Bible to the Institute whenever the owner died. When Sean explained that Tiffany was quite young and would likely use this copy for many years, "she told us we could take it with us right then!"

Actually, this Braille version of the Bible was more of a "them" than an "it"—eighteen volumes stored in three hefty boxes!

"We loaded the boxes in our truck and made our way home, numb with the excitement of what had happened," says Sean. "As we drove home, we all thought out loud about the special gift we had and how it might be received."

Then daughter Amanda, an avid reader who begs for a few more minutes each night before lights out, blurted out her sudden revelation about Tiffany: "Dad, she can read the Bible all night!"

"With that," says Sean, "we realized what opportunities lay in store for Tiffany and how fortunate we are to have God's Word so available to us all."

On Saturday, December 15, Sean, his daughters, and John Miller delivered the Bible and other gifts to Tiffany's home. Overjoyed, Tiffany right away opened one of the volumes and began reading for them.

"A four-year-old girl needed a sponsor. A Barney doll was at the top of her short list. Easy, I thought. Beckah, my six-year-old, went with me, but we couldn't find any Barney things. The clerks told us they had been sold out for weeks. Beckah said, 'Well, Mom, I'll just give her my Barney.' Suddenly she stopped and said, 'Mom, that little store down the street. I remember seeing a little girl stuffing a Barney into a toy box.'

"We hurried back, and when Beckah opened the toy box lid, there lay the biggest, plushest, softest Barney doll I had ever seen. It was their last one. 'Mom,' Beckah said, 'Jesus knew that Barney was supposed to go to that little girl. He had the other girl put it in the toy box to save it until we could buy it for her!' Thank you for giving our family the opportunity to give as 'angels unaware.'"

—*Angel Tree volunteer*

An Angel in Blue

1994

In December Janice Peek and other Angel Tree volunteers from Sardis Baptist Church in Palmetto, Georgia, made their way across the state to Claxton, two hundred miles away. Would they be able to find all the prisoners' families they had Christmas gifts for? They had only post office box numbers for several families. Would the families be willing to speak with them?

In Claxton a clerk at the Chamber of Commerce gave them a street map. Even so, the volunteers found only one street they needed. The clerk suggested they ask for further directions at the police station, where Officer Napoleon Howard met them at the door.

When Janice explained their mission, he asked to see the list of names. Then, without being asked, he led them to each home, waiting patiently as the church group delivered the gifts and visited with the children. Eventually all the gifts were delivered.

"The whole day was an experience I will never forget," says Janice, "but no doubt what I remember most is a quiet, polite angel wearing a blue uniform."

$\mathcal{B}$IKES FOR TYKES

2001

Inmates at the Minnesota Correctional Facility—Moose Lake, a medium-security prison south of Duluth, presented Prison Fellowship's Angel Tree ministry with a gift of twenty bicycles, refurbished through the prison's Offender Bike Program.

Minnesota Angel Tree Coordinator Sarah Lawrence-Wieben and her husband, Chuck, both former prisoners themselves, contacted the prison and arranged for delivery to Angel Tree children. One mother, having just been released from prison, had absolutely nothing to give her children for Christmas. Sarah heard her story and arranged for a like-new bicycle under the Christmas tree for each of the children.

Prisoners themselves developed and organized the Offender Bike Program; the repairs are made in the prison's maintenance shop. Local law-enforcement agencies, the local Munger Trail Association, and prison staff members donate the bikes, found after being lost or stolen but never claimed. All funds to operate the program are generated through the offenders' phone commission account, meaning every offender who purchases phone time donates money to this program. They also receive outside donations for bike parts— new brakes, tires, and paint—from the community, which means this program is operated totally free of taxpayer funds.

This project has the full support of the corrections

commissioner. In all, more than one hundred bicycles were donated throughout the year to various charities.

The prisoners were delighted to hear that their efforts would benefit the children of prisoners and promised to deliver even more bicycles to Angel Tree in the future!

$\mathcal{G}$IFT SHOP

2001

The story begins with Church on the Outside, a Southern Baptist mission church in Littleton, Colorado, started almost two years ago to provide a "landing pad" church for offenders being released from prison and support for the families of inmates. More than forty men and women come to the church every week for social services beyond Sunday worship. The church partners with outside agencies to provide job referrals, clothing, food, child support assistance, support programs, tools for work, and other programs to help with the reintegration of ex-prisoners.

Last Christmas the church accepted more than two hundred and fifty Angel Tree applications on its own, and then agreed to deliver gifts purchased by a suburban church to another one hundred families. Such a challenge for a new church was a step of faith, but Pastor Howard Waller, a former inmate and former Prison Fellowship staff member, never doubted the gifts would be provided. Yet even he was surprised when in September he opened a letter from Jim, a man serving a life sentence whom Waller was visiting at Limon. Jim had a young nephew who had received Christmas gifts from his incarcerated father through Angel Tree.

Jim laid out in detail how the men at the Limon prison made everything from teddy bears to wooden airplanes to clothing articles in their craft shop. Jim asked if Pastor Waller would ask the prison authorities if the men could provide gifts for Angel Tree children. A quick phone call to Chaplain Jerry Briggs put Waller in contact with the right person, who secured approval. Jim then explained the project to his fellow prisoners, and they went to work.

In early December, Pastor Waller was rewarded with the excitement of not just a couple of boxes waiting for him, but dozens! Hundreds of gifts had been carefully made by hand for the children. There were dozens of wooden toys, stitched caps, scarves and blankets, stuffed bears, elephants, and turtles. To top it off, there were seventy-five infant nightshirts.

Church on the Outside volunteers got all of the gifts delivered before Christmas. Like the fishes and loaves, the gifts seemed to multiply so that extras could be given to other needy children and some of the larger clothing items could go to recently released inmates living in shelters.

Notes Pastor Waller, "The coldness of that high-security prison, where the inmates faced a bleak and lonely Christmas, was changed forever by the love of Christian inmates who wanted to reach out to others through Angel Tree."

"Angel Tree has influenced me a great deal. It has shown me that I have a whole lot to be thankful for and just one of those things is that I am very blessed to have two great parents to look out for me and to love me.

"My mom, dad, two sisters, and some friends delivered gifts to Angel Tree children this past Christmas. At different houses, we took turns taking the presents up to the doors. It was really neat hearing the reactions of the children when they realized the gifts were on behalf of their parent who was in jail. Some of the things they said were, 'Oh, goody!,' 'From Daddy!,' and 'Yeaaaaaa!'

"But the one I will never forget was from a mother who said, 'Look, children, now we finally have something to put under the Christmas tree.'

"Angel Tree was the most exciting and touching Christmas activity for me this year. It touched my life and I am looking forward to doing it again next year."

—*Angel Tree volunteer, age 13*

Sharing the Burden

2003

In the midst of her mother's preparations for Angel Tree 2002, sixteen-year-old Marla Bristow returned home after high school basketball practice and collapsed onto the living room couch. "I am so worn out," she moaned.

Mom Julie sidled in beside her. "Let me tell you about another sixteen-year-old girl and the load *she* carries," she began.

Months earlier, as Angel Tree coordinator for the small town of Patterson in Northern California, Julie was reading over her list of 253 local prisoners' children from Stanislaus County when she noticed that three children's names were listed twice. Pulling out the corresponding prisoners' applications, she discovered that two different women—incarcerated in the same Texas prison—had signed up for the children to receive Angel Tree gifts.

One mom had listed three: Jessica, 16; Sahara, 15; and Fernando, 12. The second mom had listed those same three, plus three more: Eduardo, 8; Jose, 6; and Juan, 4.

Confused, Julie called the father in Patterson.

All six children lived with him, he explained. Years earlier, he had married the first woman, and they had three children. After they divorced, he retained custody of the children and married the second woman, who also bore three children. So

79

his second wife was mother to the three youngest and step-mother to the three oldest.

As they continued to talk, Julie decided that "both mothers had the right to give Angel Tree gifts to the children they had listed."

In November, nine Patterson churches set up Angel Trees—decorated with tags bearing gift wishes for all two hundred-plus children. Afterward, three of the tags, including one of the tags for Sahara, had not been claimed.

"On a hunch," says Julie, she phoned Jim Beamenderfer of Oracle, a large computer software company in the area, and asked if he ever donated used computers. As she went on to explain Angel Tree to him, Jim quickly agreed to provide three *new* laptops for the kids.

Excited, Julie called Sahara's dad to make sure he approved the computer gift. Sahara's older sister, Jessica, answered the phone.

But Dad was no longer there. "My father died in a truck accident last month," said the sixteen-year-old faintly.

"I was speechless!" Julie recalls. "It seemed like only yesterday that I had spoken to him."

Julie asked if there was anything she could do for the family, offering to give Jessica her phone number. But the teen declined. Everyone she had ever loved either died or left, she painfully shared. She had recently quit school and taken two jobs to help feed twelve children.

"Twelve?" a stunned Julie repeated.

Solemnly Jessica unfurled the story: A while back, an aunt with three children of her own moved in to help care for the father's six children, making a total of nine. But then that aunt passed away, leaving Jessica's dad as sole caregiver. When *he* died, another aunt—also with three children—came to live with them: one adult, who doesn't speak English, now looking out for twelve children. And eldest child Jessica struggled to do her best to help parent the others. "The family never turned to welfare for support," says Julie.

Again, Julie called Jim Beamenderfer, asking him to add Jessica's name to Sahara's computer so the sisters could share it. Jim had programmed the computer to spell out, when first turned on, "Hello, Sahara. I am your Christmas present. Take me home, and God bless you."

But when Julie met Jim to pick up the computers, he didn't have three, but *five* to give her—an additional new one just for Jessica, and a reconditioned one for Julie to use in managing Angel Tree.

At Christmas, New Hope Church—Julie's own congregation—hosted a party to distribute gifts to their Angel Tree children. Because the computers were more expensive than the gifts most of the other children received, they were set apart in an upstairs room of the church. After the party, Sahara and Jessica, along with their aunt and other siblings, trooped expectantly upstairs. They were joined by the two other children whose gift tags had not been claimed.

An extra computer sat beside the one tagged for Sahara. "Why don't you sit at that one," Julie told Jessica, "so you can help your sister."

As big sister flipped the "on" switch, "it was a *huge* surprise," notes Julie, when the screen announced, "Hello, Jessica. I am your Christmas present ..."

Later, as they all prepared to head home, Jessica's quiet

voice called out to Julie. "Can I have your phone number now?"

"We at New Hope are amazed at the burden this sixteen-year-old is carrying," says Julie. The church plans to help as much as it can, including sending several of the children to Angel Tree summer camp.

As for Julie's daughter, Marla, after hearing Jessica's story, "she became one of my hardest working and most valued helpers throughout the Angel Tree effort," says the proud mom. "We are both looking forward to doing it again. We have seen how Angel Tree touches not only those who receive the gifts, but also those who make Angel Tree possible."

"ANGEL" FINDS A HOME

1996

Carole Schmidt, an Angel Tree church coordinator in California, had difficulty reaching one Angel Tree family one Christmas. When she couldn't get them on the phone, she wrote them a letter.

Back came a reply from Effie, aunt of three Angel Tree children whose mother was in prison. Carole noted the needs of the two boys and then turned to Nichole, a thirteen-year-old girl. When asked about clothing sizes, Effie said Nichole, although very tall, weighed only eighty pounds and was fighting leukemia. What would Nichole like for Christmas? A puppy.

Carole thoughtfully asked Effie if she wanted a dog in her house, and the answer was no. So Carole went about getting the other gifts while praying about Nichole. Then Effie called Carole back. Effie had changed her mind. Yes, Nichole could have a puppy provided it was a good house dog.

When Carole mentioned the request to her pastor at Calvary Bible Church, he announced the need from the pulpit. After service, three families came to Carole with puppy offers. After a bit of discussion, Carole settled on the one that best met the definition of "house dog," a mixed Cocker-Sheltie. Then the donating family told her, "We named the puppy last week. Can you believe it? We named this one

'Angel,' and we have been looking everywhere for a child who would love a puppy."

A vet donated the puppy shots. A pet store gave free dog food, a collar, and puppy toys.

On Christmas Eve Carole was sick, but her daughter and a friend delivered Angel to a delighted Nichole. And yes, Angel was a great house dog, who loved sleeping on Nichole's bed at night with the girl.

Calvary Bible opened its collective heart to the girl. When they learned that she needed a ride to a distant hospital for bone-marrow testing, fifteen people offered to drive her. The tests were favorable, and Nichole is back at home.

Although she faces another round of chemotherapy, she does so with the knowledge that there are people in the world who care about her. Besides, she sleeps with an Angel.

Postscript
Less than two years after receiving Angel, Nichole lost her battle with leukemia.

*B*REATHLESS

1996

Chaplain Bill Moors of the California Medical Facility at Vacaville wrote that one prisoner came to him breathless with excitement. When the prisoner calmed down, he told that his daughter had just written to say she had received her Angel Tree gifts. Chaplain Moors asked what was so unusual about that.

"She lives thirty miles from the nearest town, 10,000 feet up in the Colorado Rockies and I had only a box number for her. But they found her!"

Dear Angel Tree:
"I feel really 'blessed' to have been a small part of this huge project. I enjoyed it very much. My heart was filled with joy on several stops, because of the expressions of gratitude and appreciation that were shown to us. One stop touched my heart more than words can say, but I will try to put it into words.

"I knocked on the door and didn't get an answer right away, so I knocked and knocked. I couldn't just walk away from that door. As I look back on that day, I know that the Holy Spirit would not allow me to walk away. So I knocked again, and what happened next will stay with me forever.

"Finally a little old lady came to the door and she was on the phone. She said, 'Yes, may I help you?' I explained to her who I was and why I was there and why I was knocking on the door so long. She said, 'Baby come on in, I'm on the phone with my son right now. He was checking to see if the toys had arrived.' I said, 'Thank You, Lord, for your timing.' She replied by saying, 'Praise the Lord.' I will never forget that lady's face. Her son was so happy, she told me thanks over and over. She says, her son was getting worried but, then he says God is always on time and to tell the people who are in charge of the program that he said 'thanks' and 'may God bless all of them.' From this experience alone I am looking forward to the Angel Tree project again this year."

—Angel Tree volunteer

$\mathscr{B}$EYOND THE EXPECTED

1992

Many delivery teams plan ahead to take each at-home parent or the household an extra Christmas treat. Maybe a fruit basket, a bag of groceries, stockings full of candy, handmade angel ornaments, or school supplies.

Other situations call for a church or volunteer to make decisions based on individual discretion. Along with requests for her children, one Angel Tree mother asked for a can opener. Acknowledging some "how dare she" resentment (this is, after all, a program for children), a Texas volunteer bought and delivered the best electric can opener she could find.

When the volunteer explained that the wrapped gifts included a can opener, the grateful mother acknowledged that her old opener had broken, and the only ones in the store were too expensive—two dollars.

Embarrassed to realize that even a hand-crank opener was a luxury to this woman, the volunteer asked if an electric opener was suitable. At that news the mother covered her face and began to laugh—or was it cry? Such a gift was more than she had ever hoped for. With her arthritis, using a manual opener made her hands ache for more than an hour.

PART III

WELCOMING CHILDREN

Through the ministry of Angel Tree, prisoners' families are introduced to Christians and welcomed into church communities. One Prison Fellowship staff member whose father had been in prison knows how important a Christian influence can be: "Children of prisoners are more likely than the general population to land in prison. But for God's grace, I would have been a statistic: the man behind the mug shot. I started to steal.... But my life turned a corner when I met a group of Christians willing to accept me as I was. In their care I came to Christ."

These stories show the church welcoming children—telling them stories of Jesus, giving them a loving church home, and providing role models of right living.

$\mathcal{B}$EYOND THE CHRISTMAS REACH

1996

Lueida Arnold knows the joys—and the hard work—of Angel Tree. "Of course every year I say I am not going to do Angel Tree again, but I do, because it is such a remarkable program. I get very tired, but on Christmas Day I sit home with a big smile on my face. I say, 'Lord, just thank you for giving me the health, strength, knowledge, and expertise to be able to get the children placed and get donations.'"

It's obvious that to Lueida, Angel Tree is more than a "program"; it is her passion. And it is more than a Christmastime ministry; through Angel Tree she reaches out to prisoners' children year-round in greater Cleveland, Ohio.

In 1985 Lueida was an active Prison Fellowship volunteer, concentrating her efforts on in-prison programs. "I was the coordinator of Northeast Ohio," she explains, "in charge of programming and planning." When the area director started talking about a new project called Angel Tree, Lueida jumped aboard. "It fell right into my category of 'programming.' That first year we provided gifts for six children." Ten years later Lueida oversaw gift-giving for more than seven thousand.

And an expanded ministry to prisoners' families started because Lueida—without thinking—made an Angel Tree grandmother a promise she set out to keep. In December 1991 Lueida spearheaded a team delivering gifts and groceries to "her" Angel Tree family. At the door she was greeted by a five-year-old girl who saw the packages and immediately asked if Lueida were Santa Claus.

"No," Lueida explained, "we are your brother and sisters in Christ."

Offering the gift-bearers some cookies, the child "moved in" on Lueida's heart. "I don't have anything to drink," the girl explained, "but I can give you some water."

"That really touched me," Lueida says. And so did the grandmother's request as Lueida was leaving: "I don't get a chance to take the children to church, but I try to teach them what I can about the Bible."

Lueida jumped in, "Well, you know what? We are just going to start a Bible study.

"I don't know why I said it," she continues. "But the next week, at the Angel Tree Christmas party"—at which gifts were given to children whose names had not been claimed by individuals—"I made out applications asking if parents would be interested in the children attending Bible studies. Many checked yes—but needed transportation. So we picked the children up in church vans and had the Bible study. The first night, in January, we had about two hundred children." She pauses, and then continues, expressing relief: "We had enough volunteers to handle them."

When she talks of the Bible studies for Angel Tree children—ages six to eighteen—Lueida talks about "we." The ministry is shared by volunteers from twenty-five congregations.

"We are Christians working in unity as one body. We involve the suburbs, the West Side, the East Side, all together." At an

Angel Tree party, for instance, "volunteers—black or white—come right on in and just pick up and work. We have white and black in the kitchen. We are [all] doing everything, and we are doing it together."

Team work is critical to the weekly Bible studies for Angel Tree children. "No one person is doing everything. Many people are involved, and every one of them is important."

The studies run on two tracks: Friday evening and Saturday afternoon. The first part of the study is a large-group devotional, run by a woman Lueida calls "the chaplain." "We sing and ask for prayer requests and testimonies."

Do the kids speak up? Participate?

"Do they ever," says Lueida. "They give prayer requests about teachers and friends. They give wonderful testimonies of God's work in their lives."

The children then break into classes, by ages. All the groups study the same book of the Bible—first the Psalms, now Ephesians.

"Each teacher takes a different approach," says Lueida. The teacher of the youngest class often has the children break into groups of four or five and act out a play depicting the day's Scripture. "The best group that week gets a prize."

At the end of the sessions, participants join together for an all-age discussion, led by a man who knows the Scriptures well enough to be able to field the kids' tough questions.

Bible study participants are offered a number of other opportunities—by several participating churches.

Some events are seasonal: a Valentine's Day "chitchat." "They come, and we give them little gifts and have hot chocolate and donuts," Lueida describes. "We let them express themselves." There's an Easter egg hunt. An August picnic. And "we try to give scholarships so we can send some of the kids to camp. We take them to the amusement park. We let them know that you can be a born-again Christian and still have fun."

Once a month on a weekday "family night," Bible study participants may invite their family and friends to the church for dinner, provided by volunteers. "The mothers and fathers come in and get a chance to meet the volunteers," says Lueida.

Through the Bible studies, activities, and suppers, a number of families have been drawn into the church. But church growth is not Lueida's top priority. "The whole thing is teaching spiritual insight and teaching how to accept God's blessing and how to give him something back in return." As for spiritual growth, "we do see a lot of it in the children. And some of the inmates who have come home have seen such a change in the families that they are going to church."

That kind of reward spurs Lueida to continue her ministry, organizing teams, encouraging other volunteers, presenting the Angel Tree vision to new churches.

One Family's Story
by Lueida Arnold

A young mother of four was on drugs and alcohol. She really didn't know where her children were most of the time. The father in prison signed up for the children to get Angel Tree gifts. Then we started picking them up for the Bible study. One day I took the children home. The eight-year-old girl said to me, "Mommy, would you come into the house, so you could see this lady in there."

I calmly said, "If you want to call me 'Mommy,' that is fine, but that lady in the house, she is your mother, and you must never refer to her as 'that lady.'"

I went in the house, and the girl introduced me by saying, "This is my mommy." I quickly said to the mother, "You know, we are not here to turn your children against you. We are here to try to prevent them from getting into 'the system'... I didn't realize your daughter was going to start calling me 'Mommy'; I don't have a problem with that, but that should give you something to think about. Your daughter is ashamed of you. You are supposed to be a mentor and role model to her."

She said, "Well, I would come to church if I had something to wear."

So I brought her something to wear, and when I picked her up that Sunday, she was—so drunk! I said, I am going to take her to church anyway! First I stopped and bought us some coffee, then I got her in the church. She sat through the service. When I took her home, she said, "I feel so embarrassed. When you came, I was so drunk, I knew you were going to drive away and leave me—but you didn't."

To make a long story short, after a year and a half, she joined the church. She is very active—sings in the choir. She is a recovered alcoholic; she works with me with a bilingual group. The husband is home now, and he attends church.

I admit that that first Sunday morning, I anted to beat this lady up. But the Spirit said, "Take her to church anyway." So I did.

"CAN I COME TO YOUR CHURCH?"

As told by Chuck Colson, from a "BreakPoint" radio commentary

1996

Early one Sunday morning, just before Christmas, the pastor of a small church in Oregon was putting the final touches on his sermon when he heard a muffled knock on his study door.

Puzzled, he walked over and opened the door to find three small, disheveled children looking up at him: a five-year-old boy with his three-year-old brother and a two-year-old sister.

"Mister, can we see the church that brought us those Christmas presents?" the five-year-old asked shyly.

Instantly the pastor realized who his guests were. A few weeks earlier the congregation had participated in Angel Tree, a Prison Fellowship ministry that distributes Christmas gifts to children whose parents are in prison. The three children were from one of the families visited by church members. Their father was behind bars; their mother was involved in drugs and prostitution.

"Of course you can see the church. Come on in." And the pastor led his guests around the small sanctuary. The children thanked him and waved goodbye, and the pastor returned to his sermon.

A while later, he heard another knock. It was the three

children again. "What time does church start?" asked the five-year-old boy.

"In an hour."

"We'll be back." Once again the children waved goodbye and trudged off.

Fifteen minutes later, behold, again the three children stood at the door and knocked. "Is it OK for a person to come to church if his socks don't match?" asked the oldest boy.

"Of course!" said the pastor.

The child looked up again. "Is it OK to come if you don't have any socks at all?"

"Sure," said the pastor. "Why do you ask?"

"Well," said the little boy, "my socks don't match, and my brother here doesn't have any socks at all."

"You can come just as you are," smiled the pastor. Sweeping the two-year-old up in his arms, he ushered the children into the sanctuary.

A couple sitting nearby kindly shepherded them through the unfamiliar service. But they were puzzled by a small paper bag the oldest boy was clutching. "We didn't know how long the service would last," he explained, "so we brought our lunch."

Inside the bag was a single hot dog, which the children planned to share among the three of them.

I don't need to tell you that these youngsters were quickly taken up by several loving arms and became a permanent part of that small congregation. And all because of Angel Tree, which literally opened the door to a church they never would have dreamed of approaching on their own.

This story is a powerful metaphor for the church at large.

Jesus didn't tell us to sit and wait for the world to come to us. He says, *Go* and make disciples.

This was one congregation, I'm happy to say, that didn't sit back and wait for people to come to them. Through Angel Tree, members went out and brought God's love to a needy family that might never have darkened a church door.

Their father may be in prison and their mother may be on drugs—but for these children, ever since last Christmas, there is now another world ... a world bright with God's love.

"*Why* Are You Doing This?"

1991

It didn't look much like Christmas in the warm, dry Phoenix suburbs, but members of Mountain Park Community Church in Chandler were stuffing stockings with candy and checking gift lists for Angel Tree families. As a new church, Mountain Park had eagerly stepped out on its first mission effort—giving presents on behalf of imprisoned parents to fifty local children through the 1988 Prison Fellowship Angel Tree program.

Concerned that they not miss any of the children, church members visited each home before their Christmas-week deliveries to confirm addresses and names of children. That's how a team came to knock on the door of a paint-chipped house, searching for inmate Hilario Figueroa's wife and three children.

But the volunteers didn't find a tidy household: They discovered twenty people living in a three-bedroom house and detached garage. There were Hilario's parents, Miguel and Catalina; nine of their eleven children and Hilario's wife, Anna; and eight grandchildren.

A church volunteer who understood Spanish translated the Mexican family's story. A nineteen-year-old son and a son-in-law were also in prison. Miguel and his eldest daughter, Marguerita, worked as farm tenants, and Anna had an office job, but the family income barely provided basic necessities.

The sobered volunteers reported the family's living conditions to their affluent church: no hot water; a broken washing machine; a refrigerator that didn't keep food cold—what little they had; threadbare carpet and cracked linoleum; torn couches, two wobbly tables, and four chairs; not enough silverware, plates, and glasses to go around; cardboard boxes for dressers. The children slept three or four to a bed or curled up on the living room floor in front of the only working heater. When asked how she made ends meet, Grandmother Catalina said she just worked with what she had and placed her family in the Lord's hands.

A decision had to be made: Would the church provide gifts just for the three assigned children or take on the needs of this entire family?

Under the leadership of enthusiastic Pastor Robin Wood, the two-hundred-member church rallied to the cause, collecting food, clothing, and two thousand dollars for miscellaneous items.

By December, twenty-five volunteers returned to the Figueroas—laden with cookies, gospel tracts, Christmas gifts for all, even a tree and ornaments. The church's senior citizens pitched in, providing items such as couches, dishware, and a car. A plumber and electrician donated time—to install a refrigerator and washing machine and repair light fixtures.

After Christmas a number of church members caught the vision to stick with the Figueroas, but, with turnover typical of any suburban area, that original group moved out of the picture. By the fall of 1989, new members Randy and Rhonda Wootan, who had learned Spanish while living in Mexico, accepted the pastor's challenge to coordinate an expanded

Angel Tree program for Mountain Park.

Randy took seriously Jesus' admonition to cast worries upon him; he remembers many 4 A.M. prayer sessions that fall—sitting on his front lawn, begging God to send enough helpers to provide gifts for all the children—which he did.

That Christmas a core group at Mountain Park dared ask, *Are there other families in the area that need ongoing help?* Their motto became the convicting words of 1 John 3:17: "If anyone has material possessions and sees his brother in need but has no pity on him, how can the love of God be in him?"

Since then, five needy Hispanic prisoners' families have received more than Christmas gifts and gospel tracts. Greg and Faith Wyant and their two girls have befriended Beatrice Martinez and her three children. Greg remembers the day he delivered Angel Tree gifts to Beatrice, whose apartment is just blocks from the church: "I stepped through that door, and there wasn't a sign of Christmas in the whole house. It was very bleak, and it just overwhelmed both me and my wife. We both stepped out of there saying, 'We've got to do more.'"

As Angel Tree delivery teams have discovered families living in wood shanties with no indoor plumbing or insulation, retired seniors, such as Dwayne Veith, have volunteered their home-improvement skills. Craig and Sherilyn Cooley cleared out their garage to house a well-organized clothing collection and make frequent deliveries to the families. Pastor Robin's wife, Carma, has regularly visited and encouraged the Figueroas since the church's initial contact.

Like a coach building up the team, Pastor Robin recruited professionals with hearts open to help. Dr. Merle Turner, a general practitioner and Mountain Park member, and Dr.

Kent Johansen, the pastor's dentist, have provided free medical services to more than a dozen kids and mothers, including several of the Figueroas. Hairstylist Jan McCarthy goes to the Figueroas' home to cut hair and give perms. Registered nurse Denise Petticrew conducts at-home checkups and delivers free medicines and health aids provided by the county.

Pastor Robin says the church's affluent members have had to reorganize personal priorities as they've reached beyond their four walls. "We've realized just how totally our lives had revolved around ourselves. We wouldn't even take three hours a week to change the world for someone. So it has been painful for our church members, who think we are really benevolent, to realize how unbenevolent we are." He adds that, though the church is catching on, there's always more to be done.

Forty-year-old Randy sees that cultural differences impede friendships almost as much as language. "We are WASPs." It is so uncommon for whites to enter Hispanic neighborhoods that "their first reaction to you is that you are police of some sort."

The cultural discomfort goes both ways. This year one "veteran" Angel Tree volunteer will accompany leery novices, as the growing church delivers gifts to more children of prisoners. Greg acknowledges that he feared for his family's safety the first time they entered Beatrice's neighborhood—an area disrupted by gang and drug-dealing activity.

Since the language difference prevents most of these inmates' families from worshiping at Mountain Park, Randy and Pastor Robin dream of someday planting a Hispanic congregation. In the meantime, several women are starting a

Saturday Bible school for the children, who have learned English in school. As families ask, "Why are you doing this? What do you get out of helping us?" volunteers take the opportunity to witness about Christ.

Randy is the main man who has visited the Figueroas almost weekly since 1990. When he pulls up in his white Chevy Suburban, he's greeted by a half-dozen boys—setting aside a game of marbles near the old swing set given by Mountain Park—and their younger sisters poking shy smiles from behind Grandma's skirt. They wonder if he brought along Bazooka Bubble Gum or maybe his three young daughters to run in the fields with them.

After joking around with the children, he visits with the adults. He's excited to see Marguerita's growth since committing to a personal walk with the Lord under Pastor Robin's guidance. And Randy often prays and reads his Spanish Bible with Grandma Catalina, whose humility and faith he admires. He comments, "She pulled me aside one day and told me she had been praying that someone would show up who would spend time with the kids."

Randy and Greg both hope their efforts will keep the children off the streets and out of trouble—a common problem among kids of incarcerated parents. Randy has helped the Figueroas out by talking with "tough love" to another wayward son who has been in trouble at school and with gangs. Greg laments, "To see hurting children really wrenches my heart."

Angel Tree ministry is also a great way for parents to model generosity to their own children, according to Greg. "Even my daughter, who was only three and a half last year, was wanting to give to the kids who didn't have anything."

The love of church people hasn't been missed by the inmates or their families. Beatrice cries when she talks about how Greg's family and Dr. Johansen provided food and dental surgery she couldn't afford. "They are all wonderful people. If the whole world was like them, everything would be OK."

Hilario, now out of prison and working as a welder and auto mechanic, recalls the winter of his incarceration, separated from his family: "Christmas was one of the worst days; I couldn't be with them and was far away.... When I came out I saw all these guys were helping, and that was great."

Pastor Robin has big dreams for the church's extensive ministry to prisoners' families. "We may be able to send one of these kids to college someday. We have a relationship. An agency might try to help three hundred people with something little. We are trying to help a few families have what they need."

$\mathscr{A}$ Survivor Reaches Beyond Her Pain

1994

When Ben Ratekin picked up a special order of name tags for fellow Prison Fellowship volunteers, the saleswoman Cheryl asked a leading question: "What *is* Prison Fellowship?"

Ben says he "went through the gamut" of PF programs, ending with the holiday's focus on Angel Tree—to help children of prisoners.

Cheryl paused, fingering a name tag. "My daughter Michelle was the one killed by 'those three boys,'" she said quietly.

Ben didn't need to ask who "those three boys" were. Newspapers and local TV stations had blazoned reports on the youths who—just weeks earlier—had been charged with the vicious rape and shotgun murder of a popular seventeen-year-old.

"It stopped me right in my tracks," says Ben of the mother's vulnerable disclosure. Gently he reached out and took Cheryl's hand: "How are you coping?"

Cheryl's church, Zion Lutheran, had embraced her with love and support, she explained—helping her "get through this."

Then—*right then*, Ben stresses—Cheryl picked up the nearby phone and called her church to tell them about Angel Tree. She arranged for Ben to drop off an information packet and meet with the pastor.

"I was amazed at the grace she showed," Ben recalls. And because a grieving mother's heart went out to other hurting families, Zion Lutheran "adopted" eight Angel Tree children.

"I did it for Michelle," says Cheryl of her daughter, who worked at a summer camp for handicapped kids, taught children's Bible school, and was much loved by her church family. "If anything, she'd want to think of the kids. That's why I was excited about Angel Tree."

$\mathcal{B}$ACK TO BASICS

1996

"When you don't have shoes and underwear, a toy really doesn't matter much." That's what PF staffer Jennifer King discovered when accompanying some children on an Angel Tree shopping spree at a Phoenix Kmart.

When the six Estaban* children were invited to join in the event, their young mother canvassed her neighbors, hoping to borrow shoes for each youngster to wear. Inside their small, gutted trailer, a meager pile of hand-me-downs composed the family's whole wardrobe. Four-year-old Lindy pulled out her "party dress" for the occasion: a well-worn, adult-sized T-shirt.

"They had almost nothing," says King, area secretary for PF Arizona. "Nothing but a lot of love!"

But Kmart employees, working with volunteers from local churches, were eager to treat the Estabans and other Angel Tree children to a festive Christmas celebration that included breakfast and a twenty dollar gift certificate for each child to spend on anything in the store. Most kids dashed to the toy section, grabbing Barbie dolls, Power Rangers, and assorted games.

The Estaban brood headed for the shoes and underwear.

When King and others saw what was happening, they

Family's name has been changed.

agreed to use additional Angel Tree funds to cover the children's clothing needs. Nudging the kids toward the toy section, they encouraged them to pick out something "fun." Even then, says King, the children cheerfully selected "basic things," such as paper, colored markers, and scissors.

Touched by the children's exuberance—which defied their poverty—both the Kmart employees and Scottsdale Bible Church "adopted" the Estabans. The store donated "a lot of new clothing, food, and toys," says King. The church helped locate furniture and started preparing weekly food boxes; they're making plans to send the school-aged children to Christian summer camps and vacation Bible school. The suburban Scottsdale congregation will also team up with an inner-city Phoenix church to make ministry opportunities more accessible to the Estabans.

$\mathcal{R}$ETURNING TO SCHOOL WITH SMILES

1997

"I have never seen so many people want to give so much to something like this." That's Grant Cole's enthusiastic assessment of the "back-to-school" party he organized for Angel Tree kids and single mothers in Marietta, Georgia.

Grant, a Prison Fellowship Angel Tree volunteer coordinator, ran with the party suggestion made by his pastor, Steve Brown, who had learned from single mom Suzie Hall that Christmas and "back-to-school" were the toughest times of the year for financially strapped families.

The party drew six hundred children, representing two hundred families, to the parking lot of the Milford Church of God's outreach center. Volunteer mechanics changed the oil and made minor repairs on the mothers' cars (oil donated by Quaker State, filters by Q-lube). Inside the center, Grant and his volunteers (many of them ex-prisoners, like Grant) handed out book bags stuffed with school supplies (purchased at a discount from Kmart and Big Lots stores). In another room kids fitted themselves with nice, used school clothes and shoes gathered from individual donors and through the state office of the Church of God. Other rooms were reserved for dental, eye, and hearing exams, courtesy of local health professionals. In yet another room, hairstylists gave back-to-school haircuts. Outside, bands played music, kids played basketball, and all munched down hot dogs donated by Food Depot.

"This was more fun and less stress than any other project I have ever worked on," says Grant, who felt the hand of God's blessing on the event and on his generous volunteers and donors.

NEVER TOO YOUNG TO GIVE

2002

"One-two-three—THANK YOU, GOD!" roared more than 230 children in spirited unison as they presented a six-foot simulated check to Ohio Angel Tree coordinator Lueida Arnold on the last day of vacation Bible school. The real check was delivered the next week—nearly twenty-one hundred dollars, enough to send twenty-seven Cleveland-area prisoners' children to summer camp.

"This will help make many kids so happy," Lueida praised the young benefactors of Fellowship Bible Church in Chagrin Falls, an affluent Cleveland suburb.

At the start of the weeklong Bible school, church staffer Tish Luciano presented the missions focus to the four- to nine-year-olds. "The kids were really pumped up!" she recalls. So much so, in fact, that when Tish suggested a goal of sending fifteen boys and girls to camp, the kids clamored for twenty. Some of the other adult leaders "gave me that look," says Tish, "like 'What are you going to do when the kids don't hit their goal?'" No one expected them to *surpass* it!

But Tish—whose church consistently designates a full *quarter* of its annual budget to missions—has always encouraged the kids to "get outside of themselves" and give to others. So the VBS participants went home each afternoon eager to wash dishes, rake grass, take out the garbage ... anything to earn a few more dollars for a few more campers.

One third-grade girl told Tish she had saved up some birth-day money: "Would it be OK if I give seventy dollars?" she asked.

"That's awesome!" exclaimed Tish. "But you'd better ask your parents first." The child came back with eighty-five dollars.

"*All* the kids had such a heart to give," Tish crows proudly.

Their offerings covered the fifty dollar registration fee for twenty-seven Angel Tree campers, plus the twenty-five dollar cost of giving each child a backpack filled with bug spray, toothpaste, and other camp essentials.

Next Christmas Tish hopes to join with church Angel Tree coordinator Lynn Lax to involve the kids in delivering gifts and the gospel to prisoners' children in inner-city Cleveland—perhaps some of the same ones they helped send to camp. "It's only thirty minutes away, but a whole different world to them," she says. "It will be a life-changing experience."

ALL TOGETHER NOW

2001

For years, the women's ministry at Harvest Cathedral Church had been sending boxes of toiletries and trinkets to women in prison at Christmas. But Karen Kinsler, the program manager at the one-thousand-member church in Macon, Georgia, knew there was more they could do.

So last Christmas, after much prayer and deliberation, the congregation decided to take a step of faith—by participating, at practically the last minute, in Angel Tree's Christmas outreach.

"We wanted to do more to reach families in our community for Christ," Karen says, "and Angel Tree gave us the perfect opportunity. In fact, 100 percent of the Angel Tree names that we received were right in our zip code ... they were literally our neighbors!"

In spite of the late sign-up, many church members responded, buying gifts for ninety-nine prisoners' children in the Macon area. Harvest Cathedral also managed to put together food boxes for each of the forty-eight caregivers—filled to the brim with turkey, stuffing, cranberry sauce, and dinner rolls. Then, on December 17, the gifts were laid on the altar of the church and prayed over by the entire congregation.

The next Saturday, December 23, more than thirty church members trooped out to deliver Christmas presents, food baskets—and the gospel—to their neighbors.

Assigned to the "command center" in the church, Karen watched as the different groups left for their assigned houses, filled with armloads of gifts and food. And one by one, she relates, they returned with exciting experiences to share.

Dad Comes Through

The first team, Karen describes, had pulled its car up to a row of townhouses in a seedy section of town. Drug dealers stood on the corner. Broken glass shimmered in the street.

Outside, two little boys—Quantrel and Eddie*—sat on the front stoop, fully engrossed in a heated argument. "I don't believe you," the volunteers heard Eddie say to Quantrel. "Your dad's a loser. He would never give you anything."

Quantrel's lip quivered. As he looked up in defiance at his friend, he suddenly noticed a stack of big, shiny presents—heading right to him! Quantrel ran toward the volunteers, tripping down the stairs in his haste to reach them.

"See, I told you!" Quantrel exclaimed triumphantly to his friend. "I told you my dad was going to send me something ... here it is!"

Eagerly Quantrel ripped the paper off of a box that contained a spiffy new remote-control car. "This is awesome!" he shouted, "My daddy really does love me!"

A second team rushed back to tell Karen about their reception by a grandmother, her Angel Tree grandchildren, and several relatives visiting for the holidays. After explaining the gospel to the entire family, the church volunteers asked if they would like to pray with them to receive Christ as their Savior

*All names of prisoners' children have been changed.

and Lord. "Wait just a minute!" said the grandmother. "Let me get my friend first"—and she darted across the hall.

Within minutes, the neighbor had grabbed her family and friends, too, and soon the small room was packed with thirteen people. All bowed their heads and made a first-time commitment to Jesus Christ.

As the teams returned, Karen says she heard story after story of food boxes providing Christmas dinners to hungry families; of friends and neighbors praying to receive Christ.

One team had traveled to the "Peach Orchard," the poorest, most crime-ridden part of the city. The address led them to a dingy, run-down trailer. Carefully one of the volunteers stood on the cinderblock doorstep and gave the door a firm rap. The door creaked open, revealing a small boy of about nine.

"Hi, I'm Tommy!" he said. "Won't y'all come in?" In the darkness behind the boy, they could make out nine of Tommy's relatives, all adults. Tommy was the only child in the house.

Tommy's blind, eighty-two-year-old grandmother gratefully accepted the big box of food from the volunteers. "I was going to have to decide between our electric bill and groceries," she said softly. "And now we have our Christmas dinner. Thank you!"

The brightly wrapped gifts from the Angel Tree volunteers were Tommy's only Christmas presents that year, as well as his only link to his father in prison. The family hadn't heard from him in months; in fact, until Angel Tree had contacted them, they had no idea where he was.

As the volunteers began to share the Christmas story with

the family, they realized that not one of them knew very much about Jesus. Patiently, they began to share the story of Christmas ... until Tommy suddenly interrupted.

"Hey!" he shouted excitedly. "That story is in this book I have!" Running into his bedroom, he returned waving a battered Bible. "See! It's right in here!"

Suddenly, the room came to life. Tommy and all nine of his relatives listened intently, soaking in every word of the gospel message. And when the volunteers were done, ten heads bowed in prayer to receive Jesus Christ into their lives.

Only the Beginning

The next night, Christmas Eve, Karen stood in the back of the church, listening as the thirty gift deliverers shared their stories.

A woman came up quietly beside her. "You went to see a friend of mine yesterday," she whispered. "You took her grandchildren presents. I've been ministering to her for years, and today she's in this very service. Thank you."

"Angel Tree was the catalyst for a lasting vision for prison ministry at our church," Karen says. "After Christmas we passed out the records of the families to the heads of our youth, ladies,' and men's ministries for follow-up throughout the year.

"We also mailed a personalized thank-you card to each inmate thanking them for letting us serve them and their family during the holiday season. We received many letters back."

Not only that, but this past spring, Harvest Cathedral served as the host for Georgia's Operation Starting Line, an evangelistic prison event cosponsored by Prison Fellowship. Several church members also trained to be PF volunteers, now conducting in-prison seminars for the very prisoners whose children they ministered to through Angel Tree!

This year they plan to do even more by providing Christmas cards for the parents in prison, to be given to their children. They also expect to send many Angel Tree kids to camp this summer!

"There is no doubt that God wanted us to do Angel Tree," Karen says emphatically. "It was a remarkable experience—for us as well as for the families and children who accepted Christ. I'm so glad we listened to God's urging."

"I had taken my own children with me. We got out of the car, stepped onto the front porch, and knocked at the door. Two little eyes peeked through the torn curtain, and then the child scurried away yelling 'They're here, Mommy!' The door opened and the mother and smiling kids greeted us. The little ones were probably nine and five. All four children ran to the tree and began to talk about Santa and what they had asked for. I shared some Angel Tree stories with the mother and was going to stay only a few minutes. Well, that turned into an hour. The kids found the coloring and activity books, and the five-year-old asked me to read one of the stories to her. Then she was sitting on the floor with me, listening intently as I told her about baby Jesus. We all sang, 'Away in the Manger.' My kids didn't want to go when it was time."

—*Angel Tree volunteer*

$\mathcal{M}$ORE THAN CHRISTMAS GIFTS

2000

The Calvary Worship Center in Marion, Indiana, has used Angel Tree, "a lot of ground, a lot of energy, a pond with fish, and a desire to minister to kids" to change the lives of children in their area with incarcerated parents.

As described by Pastor Jim Olinske, this small church with about one hundred members has used the day camp concept to build an annual outreach program to Angel Tree children that extends well beyond the Christmas season. They began, after a lot of prayer, during the summer of 1999 when they gleaned a list of Angel Tree children in their area for prospects.

"We contacted, explained, recontacted, and finally connected" with seventeen campers that first year, explains Pastor Olinske. The camping experience took place on twenty-six acres owned by the church, which included a large stocked pond where the children could fish and boat. Church members provided the energy, serving as counselors. One college-age member recruited several friends from school to plan and supervise the recreation. Early in the program, several grandmothers from the church noted the often meager lunches the children brought with them, so they collected food and began preparing a daily hot lunch for the participants. The children, separated into two age groups, attended six hours a day, five days a week.

The church seeks to provide a safe, fun atmosphere where the children can develop a positive attitude about the church, adults, and authority, as well as have a chance to accept Jesus as their personal Savior and Lord. The program features games, competitions, and presenters, plus an hour each day devoted to chapel. Child Evangelism Fellowship was invited to do a "five day club" for each week of camp, resulting in a clear gospel presentation.

The day camp participants also heard visiting speakers from the local police, fire department, ambulance crew, conservation department, and a police K-9 team. The fire department was the hit of the week, arriving on an exceptionally hot day. After dressing one of the campers in the heavy protective equipment worn by firefighters, the firemen demonstrated the power of their water cannon, firing water into a field that was quickly invaded by the yelling, laughing campers as they danced in the cooling spray.

Of the seventeen campers from 1999, ten accepted Christ. Calvary Worship Center then invited the seventeen kids to attend their church kids program after camp. Not only did the seventeen join, but they also brought eleven friends, several of whom have also accepted Christ. Over the following winter, ten out of the twenty-eight total were baptized in a joyful service attended by many family members.

When summer 2000 rolled around, the church had this core from the 1999 group to build on but also began contacting new Angel Tree children. Nearly eighty children in all attended the two weeks of day camping; eleven more expressed professions of faith. Many of those children are now being discipled at Calvary, and others are known to be attending regular programs at other nearby churches.

Notes Pastor Olinske, "Though a small church, we have been able—through Angel Tree—to reach into our community in ways not possible had Angel Tree not existed. We have participated in the Christmas outreach to these families for years. By being able to offer more than Christmas gifts, we see our day camp as a vehicle to permanently 'hook up' with these families."

"Praise the Lord! I would like to share the joyous experience that came to me and my family through the Angel Tree program. I have a beautiful wife and two children. I put in an application to the program so that the little ones would hopefully each receive a gift from their dad at Christmas. I called home on Christmas Day to find that a young married couple from a nearby church had come to the house in the morning bearing gifts for the children. Then my wife began to tell me how these two very nice people sat with her and the children and read to them the second chapter of Luke, from the Bible— the birth of Jesus. What a blessing! I will ever be grateful to Jesus for making that day an incredibly special one, but also to the Angel Tree program which reached out and touched four hearts that one Christmas morning. God bless Angel Tree!"

—Prisoner

THE GUARDIAN

2003

Think back for a moment to childhood, when towering old-growth trees swayed above in cooling summer wind. Smell the lake water, and feel your heart drop as you plummet to earth on a zip line. Enjoy the crackling heat of a campfire at the end of a full day.

For many a modern family, trekking into the woods may be getting harder with busy schedules and expenses. It is near impossible for kids living in the inner city who have a parent in prison. But at Camp Hope, a stunning facility set on Connecticut's largest natural lake, prisoners' kids are afforded a chance not only to experience the great outdoors, but also to hear a soul-saving message that beckons their hardened, wounded hearts.

It is also the place where an accomplished attorney found his greatest peace.

Leaving the Good Life
In 1993 Litchfield, Connecticut, was a wealthy suburb. Chris Blake was living in a big house with his wife and four children. He had switched to the Navy Reserves after many years of active duty as a JAG attorney and begun private practice in tax, estate planning, and nonprofit law. He was even a deacon at his church. His years of hard work, law school, and military service were paying dividends.

But his wife, Maggie, had begun to struggle with what it really meant to live for Jesus. She opened a conversation that Chris hadn't seriously considered. "I was a thoroughly social Christian. I had not made a heart commitment," Chris admits. A highly respected friend had noticed the same thing and invited Chris (and Maggie) to a three-day retreat at an Episcopal camp and conference center. During that weekend, God worked on Chris' heart such that he made an authentic commitment to live for Jesus, wherever that led.

The Blakes couldn't confine their faith to a socially respectable, private affair. Maggie ran across an article about Camp Hope that she showed to Chris. A week later they couldn't stop thinking about it. They sought out founder Dave MacAllister, who was building the camp on a vision and a shoestring.

The interest in Camp Hope wasn't coincidental. As they talked, Chris' past shot to the front of his thoughts. Many, if not most, of the children attending Camp Hope have a parent in prison. In 1970 Chris' own father, a lawyer, had gone to prison, devastating the family fortunes and pride. Chris remembered the stigma well. Camp Hope represented an inspiring opportunity to live out his recent commitment to Jesus and use his past to benefit a new generation. After involving the entire family in discussing the pros and cons, they jointly decided, by faith, to go to work full-time at Camp Hope.

As Chris explains, "this camp caters entirely to inner-city kids. That means [it] is always in a deficit position. No one has ever taken salaries, and we didn't expect to either." Not only no salary, but also no health benefits. Nevertheless, the entire Blake family decided to give up Litchfield's comfort and Chris' legal income for God's plan.

Of Woods and Water

Sitting on the whitewashed porch of the main camp house in July, one can view the large grass field spreading out on the west side bordered by basketball courts. A roped-off swimming lagoon, deep-water pier, and daunting high-ropes course beckon excited children. Behind the main house are nineteen boys' and girls' cabins, the "infirmary" where Maggie puts her registered nurse qualifications to good use, and a meeting lodge. The air is nearly always cool and bugless. Nature stands poised to receive the sounds of children at play.

Camping is a long way from the sealed offices of tax lawyers and military bases. "I love kids' laughter, and the fresh smell of woods and water," Chris admits. But leaving the professional life to become a camp director wasn't about some Disney dream where kids simply laugh and play to forget their inner-city lives. His mission is to show Christ's love from the moment each child steps off the bus.

Chris describes the vision: "We want to build a camping experience as though they were coming from the best suburban households rather than have it be a poor-kids' camp. [When the kids arrive] we make two long lines on either side of the bus door. As each kid steps off, we ask his name. He says 'Tyrone.' We say 'Tyrone's here!' and we all cheer. For the kid, it's like getting to the Super Bowl."

Throughout the week the children experience everything a camp should be: hikes, swimming, campfires, stories, crafts, ropes course, games, jet ski rides, and sing-alongs. Dave and Camp Hope's board of directors insist on, and maintain, a camper-to-counselor ratio of two-to-one to better "lavish love on them," Chris emphasizes. For a group of inner-city kids who've never seen camp and all its opportunities, the extra adult supervision virtually eliminates safety problems. Nationally, camps are lucky to have a seven-to-one ratio.

The four to five days go fast, and Chris doesn't waste the time. With military intensity he has his energetic college counselors drill the kids into memorizing the four most important things in the world: God loves them, they've sinned, Jesus Christ has died for their sins, and they need to decide to live for Jesus. Additionally, Chris teaches character traits like respectfulness, peacefulness, attentiveness, and others as a way of building landmarks to help carry them through when they return home.

And he doesn't oversee operations from the safety of an office. "If there's a method I run this camp by, it's pedaling everywhere and watching all the time," Chris explains. "It tells me what's going on. Noise is generally a good thing. I investigate places that are too quiet. It's an extra layer of safety. I'm watching my counselors to see if they're kneeling, and getting in the water with the children—talking with kids rather than each other. At the same time I'm watching children and how they're interacting—if there is any bullying developing, or someone's body language says they're being left out. Part of that is my military and legal training. It's inculcated discipline that really pays off in this role."

One evening after lights out, a counselor reported that "Boys' Cabin A" would not settle down, which meant that "Mr. Chris" would pay them a visit. As Chris neared, he made sure the young boys heard him stomping his feet loudly on the gravel and dirt path. He could hear them scramble to turn lights out and whisper, "Here comes Mr. Chris!" To hear Chris tell it,

I open the door, bang! and walk in. Here I am, twenty years as an attorney, as a naval officer, camp director, and father of four. I'm like God to these kids. There's moonlight coming through the window so I can see what I'm doing. I go to the first bunk ready to administer justice. I stand, looming close. I notice it's a mess—I guess it offended my Navy sensibilities. It wasn't squared away at all. I wanted to get it right. I knelt down and twisted the sleeping bag around. The lad kinda settled into that. I picked up a blanket, folded it, and placed it at the foot of the bed. I knelt next to the head of the bed and put my face close to his face. I said "Jesus loves you, and I do, too." I gave him a kiss on the cheek. I went to the next bunk, where some pants were hanging over the edge. I folded those, knelt down, said the same thing, and gave him a kiss. I went to each of those bunks, not a word being said. I just knew that's what each of those kids wanted—to be tucked in, to be told that Jesus loves them, and to have a man give them a kiss.

Changed Lives

King was the biggest boy during one session of the premium mid-summer weeks at Camp Hope. He was influential with the other kids—and a bully. It was only a matter of time before a male counselor collared young King and brought him to Chris.

"I keep going on about my current business so as not to drop everything for whatever his issue is. I tell him to sit and wait. He wants to tell me all about this big problem. I already know about this lad," he recounts. "Finally I sit next to him. He starts in, but I cut him off and ask, 'What's the second most important thing in the world?' He has to think about it ..."

"I've sinned," King answers.

"I have too. I do all the time. What's the third most important thing?" Chris continues.

"Jesus died for my sins." He knows this, at least.

Chris explains, "I'm looking at him and become aware that he's a special child. They're all special, but I speak it to him, 'I see the character trait of leadership. I see you as a leader. You have the ability to lead the children in your cabin and back in your community.'" King begins to cry. No one had ever affirmed what he suspected in his heart.

When King returned home, things started changing. His mother, who had no car, hitched a ride on the last returning Camp Hope bus of the summer just to tell Chris in person what had happened. The family had never gone to church. Now, King insisted they go and that his cousins go. That's faith having an impact far beyond one child. As Chris has learned, the inner city has a social structure of interrelated family groups. When one child goes home changed, it can and does open up entire family groups who previously were too suspicious to allow any of their kids to leave home for camp. "It's a powerful witness to them. No small part is some of the obvious class and race barriers that we've blown away. They aren't used to folks like me stepping in and loving their children. They love that," he says.

With eight hundred campers during the summer of 2002, Camp Hope is dominated by kids with a father in prison, four hundred of them steered to camp via Angel Tree. Many could go because of Rich and Helen DeVos Scholarships, administered through Prison Fellowship's Angel Tree program. Camp is also heavily weighted with boys. Another social dynamic Chris has picked up on is that the inner city will trust its sons to go to camp before its daughters. With so many fatherless boys, Chris and his male counselors have a profound influence on their lives, demonstrating what mature Christian manhood is all about.

When summer ends, the Blakes' visitation rounds begin. On most Saturdays, a list of campers in a geographic area of inner-city Bridgeport is targeted for follow-up. Chris' daughters have been particularly active in going door to paint-chipped door in search of children who need encouragement. As Hannah Blake described in an essay she wrote, "Once we've identified ourselves as being from Angel Tree and explaining that connection, [the grandmother] calls to her seven-year-old granddaughter. Out of the darkness and gloom steps Akira. We make eye contact, and she comes running straight into my arms for a big hug. I know that she remembers my friendship and my love and that we both still have hope."

The camp is also having an impact on Chris and his family. "It's caused me to parent differently and more respectfully," Chris explains. "It's more of a team effort. The 'I'm third' message they've taken to heart: God first, others second, I'm third." Daughter Kathryn seems to think her dad has learned a similar lesson, "If he could clear his schedule, he'd spend his entire day seeking God."

Looking Forward

Across the lake lies a second pristine location with dilapidated camp buildings. Camp Hope owns the property, but has yet to raise the approximately four hundred thousand dollars to bring it up to code, enabling up to one thousand Angel Tree children a summer to enjoy God's created order. Chris dreams of one day dedicating that camp exclusively for the use of prisoners' kids. He also is beginning to put his experience in non-profit law to work, organizing the fundraising and financial stewardship of the property. Summer counselors are recruited from mostly southern Bible colleges, and Camp Hope does pay decently to attract skilled young men and women. He sorely needs additional college men in order to use the full capacity of the camp and stick to his two-to-one mandate. The camp infrastructure survives mostly on local church donations, which are put to good use, but still fall short of providing a financial launching pad for improvements on the site across the lake. Were it not for the volunteer work of various church tradesmen, roofs, plumbing, and other necessary repairs would never get done.

It goes against conventional wisdom to take an accomplished Navy captain lawyer with criminal, government, and corporate expertise out of the lucrative legal environment and send him off to spend time tucking inner-city boys into bed— to be their guardian father for a week. But as Chris explains, "John Piper said, 'God is most glorified in us, when we are most satisfied in him.' For the first time in my life, I am thoroughly satisfied with where I am."

"I was one of the children to receive a gift through Angel Tree. I wanted to write and tell you how grateful I am for this gift bought for me. I really like the jeans and they fit very nicely. The eight Nancy Drew books are also very nice. I have always wanted to read them but never had the chance. I love to read, so I know they will be put to good use!

"I know that some younger children may actually think that their parent may have gone out and bought them a gift, but I realize that with my father in prison this is just not possible. So thank you again to the persons taking time and money to get me these gifts. I know my father is grateful because he does not have a chance to be with me, and even if the gifts I get aren't really from him, they still have an effect in a way. He wants to send a thank-you letter also. I know there must be many happy children at Christmas because of Angel Tree. Thank you."

—*Fifteen-year-old Girl*

$\mathcal{L}$ESSONS FROM THE ZIP LINE

2002

Chauntel chickened out on the Zip Line.

A tiny nine-year-old with a wraparound smile, she had clamored to be the first to ride the cable 650 feet down the mountain.

But she wasn't smiling now, and the other campers looked like ants far below. She relaxed her hold on the relay line and cautiously felt with her foot for the ladder behind her.

The other kids encouraged her to go for it: "Go ahead, girl. You can do it!" But Chauntel was on the ladder now, edging her way down, past the other kids waiting their turn. Then she watched as, one by one, the girls from her cabin at the Angel Tree camp in the San Gabriel Mountains stood at the top of the platform, grasped the pulley tether line, and set sail down the mountain. As each girl got off at the bottom, the pulley was pulled back to the top for the next rider.

Then there were no more kids, just Chauntel and the platform instructor. "Could I try it again, please?" she begged. He nodded for her to get back up on the platform.

She grasped the pulley tether in a two-handed death grip; she gritted her teeth and clamped her eyes shut. Then she slid off the platform into space and sailed down the line to where the others waited. Seconds later, the catchers had her and released her from the harness. Then the other girls pounced—howling, high-fiving, and hugging. Little Chauntel had just conquered her Fear of the Week.

A Church's Gift

Chauntel was one of twenty prisoners' children to discover the rigors and rewards of the mountain camp, thanks to Community Baptist Church of Manhattan Beach, California, a Los Angeles suburb. CBC has provided Angel Tree gifts for prisoners' children at Christmas for the past four years, but this was their first foray into Angel Tree camping. They scheduled a couple of weeks of fundraising to see if they could first come up with the needed funds; in less than three days they had raised enough to send at least twenty children to camp. Not prepared to start a camp of their own, CBC partnered with THE OAKS, a Christian camp and conference center located sixty-five miles north of Los Angeles and managed by World Impact Inc. The World Impact people already had eighty inner-city youth of their own coming to camp the fourth week of July, so it was easy to add in the twenty Angel Tree children.

Along with Bible studies and counseling, camp included nature classes, a variety of sports, swimming, rock climbing, camping out under the stars, and the always popular Zip Line. The Angel Tree kids had no idea what they were getting into. "I thought it was going to be boring," said Brian, 10, of Venice, California. "Boy, was I wrong! Wait until I razz the kids back home about what they missed."

What twelve Angel Tree boys from the Venice-Torrance area did not miss was sharing a cabin with a celebrity for a week. Filmmaker Dallas Jenkins, son of best-selling author

Jerry Jenkins, took a week off from his busy schedule to spend it as a cabin counselor. As Dallas glanced about Cabin 5A to check on his boys, his eyes fell on a nine-year-old who was fighting leukemia for his life. Later, at the noontime meal, the young camper stood on stage to ask God's blessing on the food, adding his personal plea for "good health for all people."

Lessons for Life

"I learned about wisdom," said eleven-year-old Pete. "I learned that we hurt ourselves and our families when we make wrong choices in life. Wisdom is learning to make good choices."

"I made a hundred new friends this week," said Deontrai, 11. "I sure want to come back next year."

"We will have at least forty kids at camp next year," predicts Jose Borges, Angel Tree coordinator for Community Baptist Church, whose leap of faith started the church down the road of Angel Tree camping.

"All of these want to come back, plus they promise to tell their Angel Tree friends. No, we will send forty kids to camp easy next year."

It wasn't easy to start with. Nearly half of the Angel Tree children invited to a free week of camping turned CBC down. "They have this comfort zone," explains Jose. "The environment most of the kids come from is not very comfortable to us, but it is all they know. They are afraid of the unknown. I'm proud of these twenty kids who were willing to chance it. They all got something out of a week in a Christian camping environment, and they will grow as a result."

Jose did not know how prophetic his remarks were. The

first Sunday the children returned from camp, eight of them, plus their parents, attended church services at Venice Beach Fellowship, a church planted in the Venice area by CBC to bring God's Word into an area Jose describes as "Satan's Stronghold."

And Chauntel has already begun to grow because of her slide for life down the Zip Line; she will be just a little less likely to back down from the next challenge life hands her.

"I have a wonderful testimony because of your Angel Tree program. Christmas 2001 was the sixth Christmas that my husband would not be home. My husband spent the last three years very far from our home here in Hawaii. Last year, however, he requested that our two eligible daughters receive Christmas gifts from your Angel Tree program.

"Our daughter Naomi was interested in 'Precious Moments.' She would draw pictures of 'Precious Moments' characters and give the drawings to her friends as gifts. She received her first 'Precious Moments' figurine from her father for a Christmas gift.

"What makes this story so special is that my husband died in prison in March 2002.... To have Naomi's first 'Precious Moments' be from her father is just wonderful. Our thanks to Angel Tree from both me and my husband. I hope that my giving to this ministry will generate wonderful stories as I have had the chance to tell.

"I am so thankful for this 'precious moment' of God's perfect provision—and for the many thousands more that your gifts and prayers help make possible. Praise God that we do not serve a random God, but One who is concerned enough to make sure that every gift is a perfect provision! May he multiply your offerings in the same way and use them to touch the hearts of many more children and prisoners with his love. Thank you, and God bless."

—*Angel Tree mother*

$\mathcal{A}$ Mother Finds Her Angel

by Maria Trubia, as told to Tawnia Wheeler

1994

Last Christmas I called to get the gift wishes of nearly fifty Angel Tree children on Staten Island. Children of prisoners. They don't open the packages in my presence. Even so, each child reminds me of a four-year-old boy named Angel, who tore open a gift under my tree, Christmas morning 1963.

Angel came into my life as a result of an offhand wish made by my youngest daughter, eight-year-old LuAnn. As she left for school on December 22, she said, "Christmas isn't fun anymore ... I wish I had a baby brother."

I sent her out the door and turned to my morning routine. But the house seemed quiet, "empty." *Maybe it would be nice having a little one around the house for Christmas,* I thought ... *Why not? Why not call Saint Michael's—a home for children from broken families—and "borrow" a child for Christmas?*

The nun seemed surprised at my request. "We have just one little boy left," she said. "All the other children have gone with relatives for the holidays, but we can't get home to our families because of him"—Angel.

Angel actually looked like a cherub with curly, dark hair and an irresistible smile. He could stay with us for three days, until Christmas night. Driving him to our house, I asked what

135

he wanted for Christmas. He had one wish: "I want to be a cowboy."

When we stopped at a store, he spotted a brown cowboy outfit with green fringes. "See!" he cried. "That's what I want to be."

Christmas morning Angel opened a mound of gifts. But he was most excited about his cowboy suit—the plastic boots and the hat that engulfed his head.

It was hard for all of us to drive Angel back to Saint Michael's. He clung to my neck and cried. I asked about taking Angel as a foster child. That wasn't possible, so I asked if we could host him for Easter. By then he was in his father's custody. I never saw young Angel again, but over the years I prayed that angels would keep watch over him.

In 1985, twenty-two years later, I heard an Angel Tree presentation at our church, Gateway Cathedral. I whispered to my husband, "Remember? We had an Angel under our tree one Christmas."

The program caught my attention, and I have volunteered with Angel Tree ever since, calling many of the 175 families our church sponsors, to collect the children's gift wishes.

I also joined a Prison Fellowship-related team that visits Arthur Kill Correctional Facility every Wednesday to hold Bible studies and counsel prisoners.

One evening I sat with a group of five inmates. I knew four of them, but one was new—and responsive to the salvation message. He accepted Christ, and I gave him a Gospel of John booklet. In the front I wrote a salutation, and I asked his name.

"Angel," he said.

I held my breath. Could this be our Angel? He has the dark eyes and curls. "How old are you?"

"Twenty-seven."

I calculated the years. "Do you remember spending Christmas with a family on Staten Island when you were four?"

His eyes widened. "Oh, yes," he said, "and the mama bought me a beautiful cowboy suit." He paused, then shouted, "You are that mama. Right?"

After that, you couldn't pull us apart.

When I told LuAnn that I had found Angel, she rushed to our attic and found a picture of me with Angel in his cowboy suit. Angel showed it to the other prisoners, bragging, "This is me with my mama."

We had been together only three days, but our family was his family.

Angel has been out of prison for four years now. He's moved away, but still sends me Mother's Day and Christmas cards.

And I still think of him when I call Angel Tree children. I see him when I walk inside the prison.

God did not give us the opportunity of raising Angel as our own. But through my work with Prison Fellowship, God granted me the privilege of ushering Angel into the family of God.

Today Angel has a son of his own. As I prayed for Angel, I pray for his family: May angels guard their steps and lead them safely "home."

"I am not sure how it happened, but a few years ago my children started receiving gifts from Angel Tree which were labeled 'from daddy.' The reason this came as a surprise was that there was a program at the local hospital that I applied for to help me buy gifts for Christmas, but this time it was different.

"They received gifts from the same church each year for almost the whole seven years their father was in prison. It was a very special time because it made them feel as if their father was actually buying them presents and they received gifts that they had wanted. The church also took time to add their extra special touch to it and buy me things as well. The Angel Tree has really been a blessing to my children and me at Christmastime and in the summer when my children attended camp at Jumonville. They looked forward to it each year, but since we moved they have not been able to attend. You have given my children a chance to experience things they would not have had if it weren't for this program. They were given a videotape of camp the last time they attended, which they proudly show when someone comes to visit. I never really got the chance to thank those involved with this program, so I hope this will let them know how truly grateful we are for your thoughtfulness and kindness during their father's incarceration."

—*Angel Tree mother*

$\mathcal{D}$EAR ANGEL TREE

1994

My brother, Jose, is serving thirty-two years in prison. He has four children, and he signed them up for Angel Tree last Christmas. He used my phone number as the alternate contact point for Angel Tree.

Before Christmas, I received a call from a woman saying she had selected the names of Jose's children for Angel Tree. After several short phone contacts, we made an appointment for her to bring the gifts to my house on Christmas morning.

On Christmas Day, I opened the door to find a middle-aged woman with bags of gifts in her hands. I invited her in, and we began to talk about Jose. I was able to share with her his recent acceptance of Christ and how he is building a relationship with God.

"I need to tell you something," she said. Her eyes filled with tears. "I know you and Jose. I saw you in the courtroom the day he was sentenced. I am part of the victim's family."

She continued, "Last month my family was at church, and we allowed our son to go up to our church Angel Tree to select the names of the children we would be buying gifts for this Christmas. When he returned and I read the name on the card, I just stood in disbelief. My first reaction was to put it back," she said.

"Then I remembered my prayers to God on the day of

sentencing. Before, I had only very bad images and thoughts of Jose, but after seeing him in person and hearing him speak, I realized that his own family were also victims in this awful situation. My feelings changed to compassion for everyone involved."

The woman said that the day her son handed her that Angel Tree tag, she cried a lot, but she could not forget that she had asked God to use her to help both her own family and Jose's to be healed. This might be the method through which God would bring Christ into Jose's life, and also into the life of her family. When she saw the Angel Tree tag for Jose's children, she knew this was not an accident. God was answering her prayers to use her.

We cried together. She is a wonderful woman who loves God and wants to be used by him. And God answered her prayer by using Angel Tree to make this happen.

Thank you so much! Not only were the children blessed with gifts but Jose, our family, and the victim's family have received a greater blessing; we have seen God's healing through the love and compassion of others.

—Tracy

"I want to say thanks. My children received their Christmas toys. As a Muslim, I don't celebrate Christmas, but it still means a lot to them."

—Prisoner

$\mathscr{A}$ Martyr's Crown for Marquis

2003

Chuck Colson tells this story:

I met an amazing young man in Philadelphia a few years ago. His name was Marquis, and his grandmother came up to me and said, "Mr. Colson, thank you for taking my grandson to Angel Tree camp last summer. He was saved there—and now he's preaching the gospel to the other kids in our neighborhood."

I talked with her grandson that day. I was so impressed—what a young man! There was a sparkle in his eye as he told me how he was leading others to Christ in their tough neighborhood.

His grandmother told me but for Angel Tree, he would have been caught up in the neighborhood gangs, doomed to follow in his mother's footsteps—straight to prison. But instead, here he was taking Jesus to the streets, sharing Christ in what has to be one of the roughest inner-city neighborhoods in America.

Just before Christmas, we received a phone call from the Angel Tree volunteers who had helped lead Marquis to Christ. The news was a shock. After walking his little brother to school, Marquis—this vibrant young evangelist—had been shot and killed on the streets of Camden, New Jersey.

Marquis was nothing short of a martyr. Although he was offered a chance to attend a private school in Hershey, Pennsylvania, he chose to remain in Camden—a very rough area. "There are so many people my age here who need help," he told his grandmother. "It's just not right for me to leave the neighborhood; they need me here."

At the funeral, story after story poured out about young Marquis and the difference he had made in the lives of people in his community—how he helped feed the poor at church, how he talked one boy out of running away and possible suicide, how he witnessed Jesus to the gangs. It was just amazing.

Our volunteers were there and offered their condolences to Marquis' grandmother. As they turned to leave, she realized then who they were and started to shout, "You see these people? *They* are the reason Marquis is in heaven. They took him to camp. That's where he met Jesus! They are the reason I have hope!"

PART IV

SHARING HOPE

The ministry of Angel Tree has survived and thrived only as volunteers and staff—church pastors and ministry coordinators, gift buyers, delivery drivers, Christmas party hosts, summer camp counselors, cooks, and directors—have caught the vision for sharing their time, energy, goodwill, and, yes, their hope with prisoners' families.

As Angel Tree is now in its third decade of ministry, some of its most enthusiastic supporters are past recipients—ex-prisoners and prisoners' spouses and children, some now grown up.

$\mathscr{A}$ Match Made in Heaven

1998

The pastor at our church saw a gift-wish tag on our Angel Tree—requesting a bicycle for a fourteen-year-old girl—and almost took the tag off, knowing it was well beyond the suggested price range. But he left it on, deciding that if it was still there after an upcoming church service, he'd call the family back and get a different gift wish.

After the service, that angel tag was gone—taken by a woman in the congregation whose fourteen-year-old daughter had been killed in a tragic school bus accident years earlier. She took the angel tag and went to sit beside her husband. She was crying and unable to tell her husband why.

Halfway through the service she wrote him a note explaining that she had found the right person to give their daughter's bike to. They had bought the bike new, and their daughter had only used it a couple of times before she died. They had been waiting for years for the "right" person. They were able to present the bike to the Angel Tree child themselves.

—Angel Tree volunteer

$\mathcal{T}$OGETHER IN SPIRIT

2003

In August of 1996, Diane Nichols of Ohio got the shock of her life. A young woman telephoned to say she was having an affair with Diane's husband, John. The woman provided such detail that Diane instantly knew it was true. Diane telephoned John. He said he would be right home.

But John never set foot in their house again. Diane's next call came from the county jail. Her husband had just shot to death the mistress who had exposed their liaison. Diane and her daughters suddenly faced a world flung upside down.

"With John in jail, I was plunged into an instant nightmare," she says. "Not only was my heart broken and my children very frightened, but I was suddenly a single mother with no means to support our lifestyle. I considered suicide, but I couldn't abandon my children."

Both girls had "a horrible time adjusting," Diane adds. "The oldest was ten and had been very close to her father. She carried a lot of hatred and pain over what he had done to our family. She was also ashamed to have a father in prison, so it made it difficult for her to function in school and to make friends."

Christmas Without Cheer

Christmas threatened to be the hardest time of all, since it had once been such a happy holiday for the family, Diane recalls.

"We would buy a big tree and decorate it together, all of us laughing as John stood on a ladder outside our house in the snow, trying to string Christmas lights. Without him, it all felt so empty. Christmas just took those hurts and made them a whole lot bigger.

"It began to be a time of dread instead of celebration."

But with John sentenced to a prison term of fifteen years to life, Diane had to get on with her own life. She moved the family to Florida, where they could share a house with her sister. She divorced John and eventually married Bobby, more to provide a father for her children than a husband for herself. Realizing she wasn't in love with Bobby but *was* in deep depression, Diane decided again to end her life. She drew up her will, leaving her daughters to their aunt and uncle. She tucked her children into bed, said a final prayer, and prepared to wash down a bottle of sleeping pills with champagne.

But before she could carry out her plan, Diane suddenly fell asleep. And though she spent a fitful night, she awoke the next morning with an inexplicable lightness. "The weight I had been carrying was miraculously gone," she explains. "I felt more at peace and rejuvenated than I ever had before, yet I didn't know where it was coming from. Then a voice whispered to my soul, as clear as if someone were speaking to me face-to-face. It said, 'Suicide isn't the way to stop the pain ... you must forgive, and then you'll be set free.'"

Diane felt exhilarated: "For once, the pain wasn't crushing me. I had no desire to die." She hurried into the children's room, shaking them awake.

"Kids," she announced with a smile, "today is going to be a special day. We are going to the store to pick out a card for

Daddy, and we're going to tell him that we forgive him." She told the girls about the voice whispering to her that forgiveness would set them free.

"I miss him," Vanessa said about her father. "I want to forgive because it will help."

"I love Daddy," added Mariah. "Can he come home now?"

Diane swallowed the lump in her throat as she held Mariah close. "No, baby. He can't come home for a long time, but if we forgive what he did and let all the tears go, things will get a whole lot easier for all of us."

In Ohio's Mansfield Correctional Institution a few days later, John wept when he received the card from his family and read its message: "As much as you hurt us, it hurts us more to not have you in our lives ... we still love you and we forgive you."

John fell to his knees in prayer. The whole cellblock could hear his sobbing.

During his incarceration, John had turned his life over to Christ and repented of his sin. Now he began to correspond with his family, sending long letters of love to his daughters. To Diane he confessed the dark secret life he had once hidden from her.

Then the family went to Ohio for five days to visit John in prison. During that time, Diane realized she was still in love with her former husband. When she returned to Florida, Bobby sensed the same thing and moved out.

Christmas of Hope
One day Diane received a letter from Prison Fellowship describing the Angel Tree program. "This is neat," she told her girls. "We can deliver Christmas presents to other children

in our community who have a parent in prison. We could share the gospel with them, pray with them, and remind them that their mommy or daddy still loves them even though they can't be here. What do you think? Should we do it?"

"Yes!" the girls agreed, so Diane sent in a request to be included as a church volunteer. Prison Fellowship asked her to be an area coordinator. It was almost Christmas, still a difficult time for the girls to get through without their daddy. But now they had something to look forward to.

"My children and I didn't get involved with Angel Tree to give to *others*," Diane admits, "but as a way of helping *ourselves* to make it through the holidays."

When they received the list of prisoners' children in their area, Diane's oldest daughter was shocked to see the names of school friends. They were kids she knew, kids she talked to at school, but she had never realized they, too, had a parent in prison. Now she felt less alone and no longer ashamed. Diane could see healing taking place in her daughter.

As they delivered Angel Tree gifts, Diane and her daughters spent time with the families, embracing single parents with their children, and grandparents raising grandchildren. "We bonded with each one because we had so much in common. No longer did my children feel different. They could hug other children just like them, who didn't have their parent at home for Christmas or any other day because of prison walls."

And Diane discovered that she wasn't alone either. "There were so many others facing the same thing, and they were in my own neighborhood! There was such joy and comfort in praying together and seeing the wide smiles on the faces of the children once they got their packages."

While Angel Tree may have been created to give to other people in need, "we found out that doing the program gave *us* something precious: joy and comfort and a whole new meaning to Christmas."

Diane, Vanessa, and Mariah have been active in Angel Tree for three years now, and each year is "a blessed experience," says Mom. "God has shown us in so many ways how important it is to reach out to others and to overcome the bad times by touching lives and making a difference. Every time we see an Angel Tree child smile, we see hope in a very hard situation.

"Having a parent in prison is a heartache that no child should have to bear, but unfortunately, close to two million children have this hardship forced upon them. By reminding them that their parent is still with them in their heart, and that God loves them and will always watch over them, it helps make the hurt a little easier to handle. Just one simple thing makes such a difference."

In June 2002, behind prison walls, Diane and John—with their daughters by their side—were reunited in marriage by the prison chaplain. "To be a real family and know that nothing will ever tear us apart again made the prison sentence, the concrete walls, the fences, and the coiled barbed wire seem irrelevant," describes Diane. "We are together in spirit and bound by our hearts through the grace of a merciful God. That's something nobody can ever take away from us."

That evening Diane and the girls went to an empty field adjacent to the prison and shot off a round of fireworks. In the distance they could see the light in a single cell, blinking on and off.

$\mathcal{G}$IVING BACK

2002

Prison Fellowship senior writer Ron Humphrey loves Angel Tree. The burly, sixty-something Korean War and Vietnam vet spent five years as the program's national director. Now, as a writer, Ron travels and sends e-mails all over the country, eagerly gathering stories of God at work in the lives of Angel Tree kids.

Just ask him about Angel Tree, and you'll see Ron's eyes begin to water as he struggles to choke back the tears.

Because Ron knows firsthand—from the wrong side of the prison wall—that Angel Tree changes lives.

For the Love of Kim

Ron met Nguyen Thi Chieu—or Kim—a young mother of eight in 1969 in the Mekong Delta of Vietnam. The widow of a South Vietnamese army officer, Kim did household chores for Ron, who was engaged in "psychological warfare" operations for the State Department and the CIA. By the time Ron's stint in Vietnam was over, Ron and Kim had fallen in love.

But Kim's work for Ron made her vulnerable once the Communists took over. Kim was arrested for spying, placed in a camp, and tortured. Hearing of Kim's confinement from overseas, Ron began working a network of connections to have her released. Finally, in 1977, the Vietnamese government expelled her and her four youngest children from the country.

Reunited with Kim in the States, Ron could not have imagined the turn his life would take. On January 31, 1978, two months after Kim's arrival, Ron was arrested for espionage.

In his fervent quest to rescue Kim, Ron had violated security restrictions. Ron's communications with a Vietnamese expatriate—who later passed on information to the Vietnamese government—posed little security risk (one CIA operative later admitted that Ron wasn't "worth prosecuting"). But in May 1978, a month after Ron and Kim were married, Ron was sentenced to fifteen years in prison.

Four years of appeals availed nothing. And in 1982, Ron arrived at the federal prison in Danbury, Connecticut—more than three hundred miles away from Kim and the children in Virginia. Cut off physically from their husband and father, Kim and the kids also suffered social isolation in a community that did not share their native culture and language.

"I worried how they would get by," Ron remembers. But unbreakable love and divine grace had gotten them through earlier horrors and hardships, and they vowed that faith and love would see them through this trial as well.

Still, as each year crawled by, Christmas was always the worst time for Ron and his fellow inmates. "You know that your family is trying to get by without you and that they don't have much money," he explains. "And you want your children to have something under the tree so that they know you haven't forgotten them."

In prison, Ron attended Prison Fellowship programs and chapel services to nurture his faith—and to temper the hate he felt toward the U.S. government. "Hate kept me going," he admits. "I told myself, I'm getting out of here, and I'm going to somehow get even."

The small but close Christian community at Danbury helped ease the anger, loneliness, and discouragement fanned by prison life. Each evening, the men gathered at the flagpole to pray. "And we had one of the greatest chaplains who ever served in prison—Buff Graham," lauds Ron. He also forged friendships with PF area director Bob Wollenweber, who led the seminars, and PF volunteer Bob Shingleton, who lived in nearby Southbury and visited Ron at least once a month.

Those friendships meant a lot to Ron, since Kim's visits to the prison were limited to only once a year. First there was the time issue: To pay the family's bills, she worked at two nursing homes, sometimes sixteen hours a day. Then there was the transportation problem: Kim's newly acquired driving skills were no match for frenzied interstate and metropolitan traffic. But once a year, church members drove her to Connecticut for a weekend visit. And once a week, Ron made a brief collect call home.

Christmas Gifts From Dad

By 1984 Angel Tree had not yet reached either Virginia or Connecticut. But when Bob Shingleton read about the fledgling program in PF's newsletter, he decided to conduct his *own* Angel Tree for the Humphrey children—all of whom Ron had legally adopted.

That December Bob and his wife, Georgiana, called Kim to find out what the kids needed and what they would like. With ideas in mind, they shopped for gifts, wrapped them, and shipped them down to Kim, who spread them under the Christmas tree to await their whirlwind unveiling.

"They knew the cards on the gifts read 'from Dad,'" says Ron. "But they also knew that 'special angels' were involved." And for the next five Christmases, until Ron's release, those special angels continued to provide gifts, ensuring the kids that even though Dad had to be absent from them, out of sight *never* meant out of mind.

Ron and Kim's church, Calvary Baptist, also came to the children's aid. The congregation owned a nearby campground, where every summer they arranged for inner-city children to enjoy a week of outdoor adventures, along with Bible studies. Ron pleaded that his children be included in the summer fun, "and my plea was heard!" he says gratefully. "They were perhaps the first of thousands of Angel Tree campers to come"—as Angel Tree Camping later officially took hold.

Return to Freedom

In early 1990, Ron boarded a bus to a prerelease center close to his Virginia home.

Ron worked for a while as a janitor at his church. "I owed them so much," he says. "Their windows and floors were never cleaner!" On March 5, 1990, he joined the staff of Prison Fellowship, where he's served enthusiastically for thirteen years—in the areas of computer technology (a skill he cultivated in prison), communications, and his beloved Angel Tree.

Today Ron coordinates the circulation of *Inside Journal,* Prison Fellowship's bimonthly newspaper to prisoners. He works tirelessly to make sure it gets distributed to more than 2,100 prisons and jails in the U.S. And as a recurring writer for the newspaper, he often focuses on issues related to veterans' needs. His stories of prisoners' changed lives turn up continually on PF's Web page and in its other publications. He corresponds regularly with numerous prisoners.

And he just can't stop writing stories about Angel Tree. Never content to simply report from the sidelines, Ron has thrown himself into summer camp activities right along with the kids (and, consequently, got thrown right *out* of the saddle of a galloping horse!).

But there's nothing Ron wouldn't do for Prison Fellowship. "Through Prison Fellowship and Angel Tree, I've been able to give back to others as others gave to me and my own family."

"Six years ago I was a resident of Metro Transition Center in Atlanta. At Christmastime I was unable to be with my family. I was very sad, because I wanted so much to give my children and my mom a wonderful holiday, but, because of my own stupidity, I was unable to be with them. My children were little girls, ages four and five. A volunteer at MTC suggested that I sign them up for Angel Tree. Just before Christmas the Angel Tree volunteers went to my mom's house to give my babies gifts from 'me' for Christmas.

"My children do not remember the Christmas that Mommy could not be with them and the nice ladies came to Grandmother's house to give them presents, but I remember, and my mother remembers. Each Christmas she and I recall what an awful time that holiday season was for us and how Angel Tree made that time a little better for the girls. I haven't been financially stable enough to share with Angel Tree in the past, even though I have been longing for the time when I could. I often think of the children of present inmates who don't understand why their mommy or daddy can't be with them at Christmas. Who cares for these children, loves them, and provides gifts for them? I believe God uses Angel Tree to show the families of inmates that someone really does care for them.

"My prayers and support are with you. Enclosed you will find a check to provide Christmas gifts for two children. Thank you, Prison Fellowship, for the priceless gifts you gave to my own two babies at Christmas, and may God bless you."

—*Ex-prisoner*

*F*ORGIVING THE UNFORGIVABLE

2002

Karen Radcliffe had a simple reason to deliver Christmas gifts to the children of a certain prisoner named Jay*: "I just want to tell them the Christmas story," she said. "I want to bring God's love to them."

What was not so simple was the courage she summoned to deliver the gifts. You see, Jay was an accomplice in the murder of Karen's husband.

Nearly a year before, one wintry January night in 1991, Karen was watching the eleven o'clock news when her husband, Bill, called. Pastor of a small church outside Lafayette, Indiana, he had driven down to Indianapolis to visit a hospitalized member of his congregation. He told his wife his Chevy Cavalier had overheated, so he'd probably have to stop a few times along the interstate to refill the radiator. "Don't worry if I'm late," he reassured her.

But Bill never made it home. At a roadside rest area, where he'd stopped to refill his water jug, two men robbed him, and then one shot him in the back of the head. A trucker found him on the floor of the rest room.

When the police notified her, "I went right into a crisis mode," Karen says—riding with friends to the morgue to identify the body, explaining Bill's death to their twelve-year-old son,

Name has been changed.

157

Matt, making funeral arrangements. She warned the minister, "I don't want to hear any of that 'God's will' or 'everything works for good' stuff." She wasn't angry at God—*"He* didn't do this." But her husband was *gone.* She just wasn't ready for platitudes.

Three months later Karen opened her newspaper to confront the photos of three suspects arrested by police. As she stared at their "scruffy faces," the combination of Karen's Christian compassion and social-work experience led her to speculate about their childhoods: *What horrible circumstances had helped mold such violent characters?* Even so, Karen insists, "every person is still responsible for the choices he makes." But she softened at the thought that these men had probably never heard about God; "that the closest they had ever got to religion was killing a pastor." She envisioned that once they were convicted and behind bars, she would ask the prison chaplains to meet with the men. "I had this fantasy that the light would come on and they'd all accept Christ," she chuckles.

Gift of Forgiveness

One of the defendants, Jay, whose own gun had jammed during the robbery, agreed to a plea bargain of fifty years in prison in exchange for testifying against Gerald, the triggerman. After the sentencing hearing in October 1991, Jay asked if he could speak with Karen. "You don't have to," police officers assured her. "But I remembered my plan to call the chaplains," she says, "and I thought, *If I refuse to talk to this man, it will be a rotten example of anything Christian. And the chaplain won't stand a chance.*

"I wanted something good to come out of this," Karen continues. "And I knew this was something Bill would have done.

I wasn't betraying him in any way."

Jay shuffled over, his feet shackled, his hands cuffed in front of him, a long chain secured around his waist. "I'm *so* sorry," he grieved.

"I am, too," Karen answered, thanking him for his upcoming testimony. "It's hard, hard for both of us," she added as she noticed a tear sliding down his cheek. Instinctively she reached out to touch his arm. "I'll pray for you," she added. "Will you pray for me?"

Startled by her request, Jay agreed. Then officers escorted him away.

In February 1992, a jury found Gerald guilty of murder and sentenced him to death. At the advice of the prosecutor, Karen turned down Gerald's request to speak to her *before* the sentence. Afterward he didn't ask again. But Jay sent her a note, underscoring his regret for his part in the killing: "Every single day I feel your loss." Since then Karen and Jay have continued to correspond; Karen sent him a Bible.

Drawn to Life

In September 1992 Jay committed his life to Christ, in the presence of a visiting prison volunteer. Later he made a video of his testimony, crediting Karen with helping lead him to salvation. "Mrs. Radcliffe is probably the most amazing person I've met in my life," he marvels. "I never thought you could hurt somebody so bad and take somebody they loved away, and they could forgive you for it. She reached out and held my hand and said, 'I forgive you.' I had never experienced any kind of love like that."

Karen shares her honest feelings with Jay, so that he understands how deeply she and her son feel the painful loss of her husband. She still weeps when she thinks of how Bill's death robbed her son Matt of his best friend and biggest cheer-leader, and caused him to be "ticked with God." She finds that her ability to be open with Jay has contributed to her own healing. "He's one of the few people I can really talk to about what happened—because he was *there.*"

Having shared Christ's love with Jay, Karen turned to share that same love with his children. "One time I read something about Angel Tree and thought, *What a good idea!*" So she made arrangements, with the permission of Jay and the children's grandmother, to deliver Christmas gifts.

Once, Karen wrote a letter to Gerald, on death row in an Indiana prison. In it she shared her own situation of being at death's door several years ago with metastasized cancer. She remembered the terror and anguish she suffered—and the peace that Jesus brought her. "I just want him to know that he doesn't have to die alone," says Karen. "And I don't want him to die thinking I hate him."

Postscript 2003

Since this story was written in 1992, "Jay" was paroled but is now missing and in violation of his parole. A prison chaplain said that Gerald accepted Christ shortly before his execution by lethal injection in 2001. Matt Radcliffe is now twenty-four and preparing to marry. His mother remains at the family home in Indiana and holds no bitterness toward Jay, praying only that he will be located before any harm comes to him.

"Seeing three churches, who have long avoided contact with each other over 'membership poaching' issues, join together to put on the Angel Tree Christmas party brought tears of joy to my eyes! The party was held at a roller skating rink where more than forty children, including thirty Angel Tree children, joined together for an evening of fun. The youth group from one of the churches did the gospel presentation via a puppet show, and it was the hit of the party.

Another exciting part of Angel Tree came from church members sending Christmas cards to the inmates whose children were served. I have received tearful phone calls from some of those members who were so blessed by the heartwarming responses from the prisoners. I see a real possibility for people to catch a glimpse of the vision of having an effect on the crime rate here through Christian love. It is not going to happen all at once, but I believe it will."

—*Angel Tree volunteer*

CATCHING THE ANGEL TREE SPIRIT
1989

In Greensboro, North Carolina, the Angel Tree spirit, caught by thousands of children and volunteers, has been fanned into a fire by a woman named Suzan Rand. If you ask just about anyone connected with PF in Greensboro how he or she got involved, the answer is likely to be, "Suzan called me."

Run after Suzan long enough, and you'll see her all over the city, hugging an inmate's child, grabbing the hand of a store manager to tell her that the mall Angel Tree will be arriving soon, persuading the mayor to institute a city-wide Angel Tree Day, driving her daughter to a flute lesson, waving and calling out to the street people by name as she careens on one-way streets.

Energetic Suzan, volunteer coordinator of the area's Angel Tree outreach, has flaming red hair and a life to match. In Washington, D.C., in the early 1960s, she worked for the CIA during the day and test-drove Goodyear tires at night. She cleaned airplanes; she served as marketing director for a Swedish company handling organ transplants. In the late sixties she did paralegal work at Gadsby and Hanna when one of the firm's partners, attorney Chuck Colson, went on to work in the Nixon White House.

Today you won't find Suzan Rand testing tires, shipping kidneys, or vacuuming jets. She is still a legal secretary, however—in Greensboro, where she and her family moved in December 1984.

Suzan had worked at Prison Fellowship's national office for five years, growing increasingly excited about Angel Tree, which serves as a doorway to long-term ministry to prisoners' families.

So even while Suzan and her husband, John, were unpacking boxes, Suzan already was examining her Greensboro map to see which of the ninteeen nearby prisons was most accessible. It was Sandy Ridge, and Suzan called the chaplain. Within twenty-four hours she had a list of children's names.

Next she called Christ Covenant, a church near the prison; within twenty-four hours an Angel Tree was set up in the narthex, and by the following Sunday members were buying presents. By Christmas Day, 250 children were ripping open unexpected gifts from their absent fathers.

It was a whirlwind, atypical Angel Tree, but the results were not: Inmates' children saw the love of Jesus through the outpouring love of his people.

Sandy Ridge Chaplain David Fleming sees the effects Angel Tree has had on prisoners: "They feel overwhelmed and surprised by the compassion and love of the Christian community. They've had religion preached to them, but a lot of them haven't seen real Christianity lived."

Real Christianity lived is what Suzan Rand is all about. And her energies have sparked a variety of outreaches to needy children.

In 1986 Suzan asked her former boss, now state representative, Trip Sizemore to adopt one prisoner's three children—angels on the mall tree. Sizemore quickly obliged, buying gifts and even driving two hundred miles to pick up the children, whose mother was incarcerated in Raleigh. The plan was to bring the children to the Greensboro mall, where their presents—and another surprise—awaited.

As the children eagerly walked toward the Angel Tree, their mother, furloughed for the day, ran toward them with out-stretched arms. The reunited family—and the curious onlookers as well—cried for joy.

Since then Trip Sizemore, now chairman of the state cor-rections committee, has become increasingly involved with PF's outreach to death-row inmates in Raleigh. In recent death-row seminars, Trip, PF North Carolina Area Director David Haley, and other volunteers have fostered relationships with many whose days are numbered.

And Suzan Rand has garnered help for those men's chil-dren—from First Presbyterian Church of Greensboro, about as far from death row as one could get. The old turreted brick structure with high rose windows sprawls over a downtown city block. At Suzan's request, the church has given several thousand dollars each year as a resource for both Angel Tree gifts and sum-mer camp scholarships for the children of death-row inmates.

On yet another front Suzan and the Greensboro Angel Tree have reached out to the family of Brenda Gattis, a hosiery fac-tory worker. Brenda's framed marriage certificate hangs on the wall in the bedroom of her housing-project home. In a door-way dangles a stained-glass mobile listing the fruit of the Spirit.

Faithfulness and patience are chief among Brenda's virtues; her husband, Billy, has been in and out of prison, mostly in, for thirteen years. Brenda has held her family of seven chil-dren together with discipline, determination, and Christian commitment.

For five years Brenda's children have received Angel Tree gifts, but Angel Tree means more than Christmas to Brenda, as she discovered through a summer afternoon tragedy in 1988, when her seven-year-old daughter, Jamie, was hit by a car. At Duke University Hospital Brenda and furloughed Billy watched as doctors removed life support equipment and Jamie stopped breathing.

"After Jamie died, the devil tried to steal all my hope," says Brenda. "But I focus on the Lord. I couldn't have made it without friends like Suzan Rand who stood with me. Through the help of the Lord and people who love the Lord, we're doing real well."

From his prison cell, Billy also thanks Angel Tree. "I didn't realize what Angel Tree could mean until I saw all that these people did. They were sent by God to help my family during a time of crisis and to be our friends."

Perhaps William, Brenda's oldest son, learned this most strongly last summer when Christians from the Praise and Worship Center, a new storefront church in town, gave him a scholarship to a Christian sports camp.

But when he received a camp information packet, William's hopes were dashed. He saw pictures of kids horseback riding, swimming, diving, climbing. But there was also a list of items to bring: flashlight, warm jacket, t-shirts ... things William just didn't have.

"I've got this present," he complained to Suzan Rand, "but I won't be able to use it."

"Well," responded Suzan, "I don't know what you're going to do, but I'm going to pray that God will provide those things for you."

"Oh, yeah?" challenged William. "How's God going to get it here?"

William should have figured that Suzan had a pipeline to God—and his people. She made William's needs known to the tiny Praise and Worship congregation, which took up an offering and sent their pastor's wife shopping. By the weekend Suzan Rand returned to the Gattis home with the listed items and more.

Struggling, William told Suzan, "They got that stuff because they like you, not me. They're white and I'm black. They're rich and I'm poor."

"William," said Suzan, "for starters, these clothes don't fit me. They got them for you. They care for you, whatever color you are. And they're not rich: This is a little church, and they had to dig deep so you could have these things."

With that, William understood that Christians did care—all year long.

Suzan takes no credit for the success of Greensboro's Angel Tree: From the day after Thanksgiving until Christmas Eve, a band of volunteers meets to pray from 5:00 to 6:00 A.M., committing every facet of the project to God. Suzan says, "God just thinks about these things. Then he dumps his ideas on me, and I'm ready to respond."

$\mathcal{A}$ NETWORK OF GRACE

1994

In her fleeting twenty-seven years, Marianne Bullock paid dearly for her extended rebellion into drug use and prostitution. She'd spent several stints in jail and prison. She'd contracted the HIV virus. She'd birthed—and lost—a baby with full-blown AIDS. Now she was back in prison. Squarely facing an ugly death. Halfway across the country from her two children, who lived with their grandmother.

And in those last months of Marianne's life, a Prison Fellowship cross-country network rallied to respond to a series of urgent "can you help?" requests.

Late in 1993, Marianne, a Blackfoot Indian, made her petition to God himself; at a PF In-Prison Seminar in a Louisiana prison, she asked Christ into her life.

She also filled out an Angel Tree application. That request—that her children in Washington State receive Christmas gifts bought by church volunteers—set the interstate network in motion.

Shirley DeLoach, then PF area director for Louisiana, sent the application to the PF Washington office, which assigned the children to Angel Tree volunteer Steve Haines. Steve delivered the gifts—and an offer—to Marianne's adoptive mother, Catherine Forinash: "Call us if you need help."

And in May, Catherine rang with a specific request: Could

PF Washington Area Director Dick Cinkovich ask someone in Louisiana to visit Marianne immediately? "They weren't sure she would live into the weekend," Dick says.

It was Dick's turn to call Shirley, his Louisiana counterpart. "Can you help?" he asked.

Shirley agreed to make the contact herself, as she "happened" to be going into that prison the next morning.

Bedridden in the infirmary, Marianne voiced a desperate plea: "Can you help me not to die in prison?"

With Marianne's sentence—and earthy life—near an end, Shirley couldn't say no. She started working local, state, even national, connections: social services, the Department of Corrections, the Federal Bureau of Indian Affairs. In the Northwest, PF staff and volunteers worked with a local Christian AIDS ministry to line up an air ambulance and a doctor and nursing home willing to accept Marianne's case.

Though the red tape took two months and the release required the governor's signature, in July a skeletal Marianne flew across the country. "Realistically she should have died before the paperwork was completed," notes Dick. "She must have had a strong will to live and see her family.

"She was in Tacoma a week before she died," Dick continues. There she saw her children and died in the care of her mother, graced by a network of Christian friends who were there to help when heaven drew near.

FROM THE MIRY CLAY TO THE STEADFAST ROCK

1998

Pancakes devoured, spilled milk sopped up, the children stream out of the cafeteria and head for the grassy athletic field: site of the morning's summer-camp games. On the way many of the kids vie for a chance to "hang" with camp counselor John Baker, who always greets them with a broad, affable smile.

He loads one youngster on his back and grabs the hand of a chubby little girl who tends to stand shyly on the sidelines. "Being with the kids is a blast!" exclaims John, as he trots toward the relay races.

The next morning a more sedate John stands before his youthful "congregation," as he speaks during the camp's Sunday worship service. "There are some places so lonely that you feel you just can't make it," he says to the campers. "When you feel that way, reach out to God. Think about how much he loves you. And we love you, too."

Later, out of their earshot, John talks about the kids—all children of prisoners, attending a Prison Fellowship Angel Tree camp. "Children are so often forgotten in the mess of prison," he says. "Most of them need a father figure really, really badly." Many have been abandoned, neglected, abused. "If they don't have a parent around, they're going to go looking for someone to take their place. And if we don't reach them with something positive, they're headed right down the same road"—toward crime and prison.

So John reaches out with lavish love. "I'm unreserved in showing affection and care. As long as they know that someone is there not to hurt them, but to *be* there for them, it's easier for them to trust." Many of the kids, John notes, "carry around a lot of pain and fear."

John knows all about pain and isolation. "When I was a kid, I needed a lot of attention that I didn't get," he explains. Though he knew his parents loved him, both seemed uncomfortable expressing their feelings. That trait passed down to John, who concealed his own emotions when they most needed exposure. "I was afraid to show who I really was," he says. "That's why I'm so motivated to work with these kids."

John also knows prison life. After each day of camp activities—unlike the other counselors—he has to take the ninety-minute car ride back to the Community Corrections Center in Lincoln, Nebraska, where he's serving a twenty- to eighty-year prison sentence. He's been incarcerated since 1981.

"I think if I'd had some special attention as a kid ..." he begins—but the conjecture trails off unfinished. He remembers life's mud-caked road: severe learning disabilities that put him behind the other kids and sapped his self-confidence; his attraction to other "social outcasts"—"since that's how I felt about myself"; his increasing use of "escape" drugs—marijuana, LSD, PCP, and cocaine. By his late teens, John had plummeted into a depression and self-loathing that drove him to take off by himself for days at a time.

"I'd drive to the lake and pitch a tent," he says. "I isolated myself from everybody; I talked to myself a lot"—but not to anyone else. Concerned, his sister once probed, "John, what's wrong? What's going on with you?"

"But how could I put into words something I didn't understand myself?" asks John two decades later. "I was scared. I was angry. I was numb. There was no meaning; life was just plain dead. I wished I could have told her all those things, but it was all just too confusing. It was like everything was swirling around me, and I couldn't catch hold of anything."

What eventually happened, John tries to frame in similes: like a clumsy child who can't get his toy truck to "work right," so he slams it against the wall; like a frazzled woman frustrated about her workday, so she slaps her boyfriend. Finally he discards the frames to expose the stark and brutal reality: the twenty-one-year-old son who shoots his sleeping parents in a spasm of rage, "not out of anything they did to me, but out of something I felt toward myself," he says quietly. "It was sick; it was horrible."

His youngest brother, Jeff, then only a high school student, found his bloodied parents in the bedroom—his father dead; his mother fast losing her hold on life. John attacked *him*, too, but Jeff fought him off.

Pleading guilty to two counts of second-degree murder, and deemed a paranoiad schizophrenic by the judge, John was sent to a maximum-security prison.

Drawn by Love

Locked down twenty-three hours a day, John spent his hour of daily "free" time circling the prison's outside basketball court or playing Ping-Pong and watching TV. "I was getting really stir crazy," he describes.

Then he noticed that a fellow prisoner got additional time out of his cell on Friday evenings. "Where do you go?" John asked curiously. To a Christian Bible study, the inmate answered. And if John signed up, he could come, too.

"I jumped at the chance to get out of my prison unit," John recalls. "In prison, little freedoms are huge!"

Six church volunteers led the study, "and when I walked in, I was instantly accepted," John says. "It didn't matter who I was, what I had done. I saw the love they had for me. And I felt safe."

That security drew him back week after week. "I learned what unconditional love truly is: that Jesus Christ loves me no matter what I did. That God would forgive me, no matter what. I had murdered my parents, and yet these volunteers saw me as a child of God, someone of value that God had made. I was not a monster." Finally—gratefully—John received God's forgiveness and turned his life over to Jesus.

Transferred to another Nebraska prison, John attended every Bible study and Christian program available, including many led by Prison Fellowship. "Those volunteers!" he says. "Those are the people who brought Christ into prison and enabled me to find who I truly am."

Assured of God's forgiveness and healing, John worked hard with professional therapists to examine and understand his past. "It was really difficult to take an honest look at what I had done," he says gravely. "I had to do it in steps, over a long period of time."

But particularly with a Christian psychologist, "someone I could trust, who made it really safe," the disclosure was "unburdening," he says.

At the same time, John threw himself into every other positive opportunity to keep his mind and body active—and focus his attention on a sound, steady future. For eight years he worked in the prison warehouse, developing a "good work ethic." Another prisoner taught him leathercraft. After a deaf inmate came into his unit, John and several others took an eight-week class in sign language, conducted by a volunteer. "All of these things were another type of freedom," he says.

John and his fellow Christian inmates formed a close-knit community. Through achievements and setbacks, "we were always there for each other," he describes. "I developed some really strong friendships." That special bond also extends to certain PF volunteers—such as Nancy and Larry Carlson, who have known John nearly his entire time in prison. "If you say prisoners can be rehabilitated, John is the one you can say it about," says Nancy. "He's not the same person he used to be."

Prison staff also noted the change. Former superintendent David Avery called John "a model prisoner the whole time." A few years ago officials allowed John to skip over several security levels directly to work detail—leaving the prison grounds daily to work at a full-time job in the city.

"I was so amazed when I got the job!" John says with excitement. "I know God's hand was in it."

Steps to Reconciliation

God's hand has also touched the lives of John's family members and former neighbors, who were hurt and horrified after the murders. His sister Julie, who turned to Christ shortly after John did, "was always there for me. She believed that something had to have been really wrong with me to do what I did."

Julie, away in nursing school when she got the phone call about her parents' murder, admits her feelings vacillated dramatically. "I was enraged, confused, brokenhearted, despairing," she recalls. Nevertheless, "I knew I loved John dearly, and my love wasn't going anywhere."

Afraid she would have trouble forgiving her brother, "I turned to God right away—'Please help me do this.'" At her priest's encouragement, she expressed her feelings honestly each time she visited John in prison, "so we could deal with them as they came up." The whole process of forgiveness, she says, took about two years.

Since John's imprisonment—and particularly since his conversion to Christ—"I've seen him go from a crippling mental illness to mental and spiritual health," says Julie. As John enthusiastically shared the lessons he'd learned from the Bible, "I started learning from him. He's been one of my best teachers."

For several years, brothers Jerry and Jim refused to visit John in prison. Now both have reestablished contact and expressed forgiveness.

Youngest brother Jeff remains angry and distant—"which is understandable," John concedes sadly. "He was still in the house when everything happened. He had to fight for his own life. He had to call 911. He had to get my mother to the hospital"—where she soon died. "He was severely traumatized."

At John's first parole hearing in June 1997, seventeen people spoke in John's behalf. Jeff brought along twenty-three people to oppose early release. "They had never had a chance to speak publicly about how they felt, the pain I had caused," says John. "Now, after sixteen years, they could let it all out. I think God used the hearing as an opportunity for healing."

His sister remembers that day, which ended with a denial of parole. "I watched the tears streaming down John's face as each board member told him they couldn't support him at this time. Yet he sincerely thanked them for the opportunity and told him he respected their decision. I sat there in awe at his reaction."

John continues to pray for reconciliation, which he deems more important than his release. "God has done so much for me," he praises. "Why should I get discouraged? For my brother and the other people—the ones who were hurt the most—I need to stay in prison for now ... I would like to get out soon, but God is at the helm."

John reflects on where he was, where he is now. "I miss my parents," he says, his eyes tearing behind his glasses. He recalls his dying mother's last words to the family: *Please forgive John.* "I am so sorry for what I did to them, and I believe they have forgiven me, looking down from heaven.

"I think they would be proud of me now," he adds. "How I've changed through God's love and forgiveness. And for the rest of my life, I want to live up to their pride."

For the rest of this camp weekend, he plays among the Angel Tree children, giving out affectionate hugs, laughing his way through "motion" songs that test his dexterity, joining in friendly splash fights in the lake, listening when someone just needs to talk. "It's great to be out here with the kids, having fun," he says. "And if I can help redirect a kid who might be going down the same miry road I was headed down, that's a real joy."

Postscript 2003

Now forty-three, John has spent more than half his life in prison. In 1999, two years after this Angel Tree camp experience, John was transferred to a work-release program at the Community Corrections Center in Omaha, Nebraska. Doing "grunt work" at first for a local law firm, he soon demonstrated a natural aptitude in computer skills—which he has augmented with college classes. John is now close to earning his associate's degree in computer network technology and has steadily gained more responsibility in maintaining the firm's expanding computer network.

He still stays in close touch with Prison Fellowship volunteers Nancy and Larry Carlson. Unfortunately, his transfer to Omaha put an end to his participation in the Angel Tree summer camp near Lincoln—"but I'm eager to work with the kids again!" he says.

Angels in Venice

by Ray Allen

2001

It was a cold winter evening in Venice, California. The dense fog had rolled in hours before, covering the streets with moisture, making them slick. We drove along Lincoln Blvd. passing Washington as our police radio screeched, "14A01 Man down in the alley, Brooks and California, shots fired, possible gang activity. Handle the call Code 3."

My partner "rogered" the call as I flipped on the red lights and siren. Accelerating toward Brooks and California, I struggled to see and keep the car in a straight line. The eerie red glow from the lights was thrown back by the fog, and the wet streets made it a more harrowing journey. We slid to a stop and fought our way through a group of racially mixed youths standing over the fallen warrior who could not have been more than fourteen years old ...

For Angel Tree volunteer Ray Allen of Community Baptist Church in Manhattan Beach, California, it was a twenty-five-year-old flashback. Recently, the former Los Angeles police officer found himself delivering gifts on the same mean streets he once patrolled as a cop. Here's his story:

African-American and Hispanic families began moving into Venice, California, fifty years ago to escape the crime, drugs, and violence of South Central Los Angeles. Sadly, they merely

177

imported into Venice the problems that plagued them in South Central.

One area of Venice, known as "Oakwood," housed the majority of our Angel Tree children. Oakwood is named after the city park. Unfortunately for the children of the area, ethnic gangs maintain control of Oakwood Park. Many turf battles begin there and spill out into the nearby streets and communities.

Having worked this area in the early 1970s with the Los Angeles Police Department, I felt that my perceptions and street knowledge would help our church in getting the Angel Tree gifts safely delivered. As I began to walk the streets of Oakwood again—this time as a volunteer bearing gifts and the Good News—I had flashbacks of radio calls and experiences from twenty-five years in the past. Visions of gang members on the street corners, drive-by shootings, drug sales, and vehicle and foot pursuits through the courtyards of government housing tracts.

At our third stop, I walked up to the front yard fence of the single-story yellow house and unlatched the front gate. I checked for dogs. Then we knocked on the front door, and a female voice answered from within, "Who is it?"

I replied, "We are from Angel Tree, and we have presents for the children." Slowly the door cracked open and the occupant carefully surveyed us standing there and holding the brightly colored presents for her three children. Finally the door was fully opened, and I observed a middle-aged African-American female, dressed in gray khakis and a black Oakland Raiders jersey.

The lady listened hesitantly to us at first, and then explained that only two of her three children were at home just then. When we told her that we just wanted to be sure that the children received the gifts from their father, her eyes widened and a slight smile came over her lips.

I now read the greeting on each package to the children who were present: "I love you all so much and will see you soon. Love, Dad." Now the woman's smile was from ear to ear, and the children quickly claimed their gifts.

One of our team members, Amy, asked her a few questions and found the woman would be willing to host a small home Bible study. We took pictures of the children's beaming faces and held hands in a small circle of oneness to pray for the family.

As we were just about to drive away for our next stop, the lady came running out to our truck with a huge twenty-five-pound frozen turkey. She pushed it toward me and said, "I have two, and I just want you to give this to someone less fortunate." She thanked us and walked back into her house as the children waved to us.

The next stop was just a few streets away. We searched for the number "657" on the houses, as well as parking spaces. Then we knocked on the front door of the nearest house. A man answered our knock and told us that the address we were looking for was behind his house; we needed to enter through the alley. As we did, it flashed upon me that this was the same alley where my partner and I had found a gunned-down youngster twenty-five years earlier.

We passed the rear of two houses, and as we came to the third structure, we noticed "657" spray-painted on the exterior of an old wooden garage. We knocked on the gate, and a gaunt-looking Hispanic lady came out. We told her that we were from Angel Tree and that we had gifts for the children from their father. As we entered we noticed that the residence was a converted garage with a vegetable garden and outside cooking area. It was like stepping into a third-world country.

Children began to appear as we walked toward the open door. The poverty of this family was striking as my eyes glanced around the humble dwelling. I gave the lady the turkey from our previous stop. She was overcome with joy and said that now they could have a Christmas dinner.

We asked if we could pray with their family. As we joined hands in a circle of grace and thanks, I could see that the gift of the turkey and the last two deliveries were not a coincidence. God had worked a miracle for this family with the turkey, and we were all instruments of his grace.

As we quietly walked back toward our truck, I reflected on my time spent in Oakwood twenty-five years ago and today. God is the bond between generations and all races. What a gift you have given me this Christmas, Lord!

"Every year our church participates in your Angel Tree program. Members purchase gifts and deliver them to children you have assigned to us.... This year, instead of purchasing a gift for a child, I decided to use my hands as well. I made twenty-eight Christmas tree ornaments and sold them at my place of employment, a Christian bookstore. Thanks to the customers, twenty-three of the ornaments were sold for a donation of $5 each. Enclosed is a check for $125 which is the total that was raised. I truly hope this contribution helps a few children find happiness. May God bless your work."

—Angel Tree volunteer, age 16

"Not an End, but a Great Beginning"

2002

A sudden mid-afternoon windstorm sprang up and threatened to blow the mountain over. Then it died down as quickly as it had begun; two large fans were switched on, and the portable mountain rock-climbing wall, now standing in a prison yard nestled in the shadows of real fourteen-thousand-foot peaks of the Colorado Rockies, slowly reinflated.

And just in time. The first half of the sixty-six blue-shirted youths in the nation's first Angel Tree camp inside a prison— "Adventure on the Hill 2002"—were now filing out of the prison auditorium. With great anticipation and a little nervousness, they readied themselves to challenge the forty-foot canvas-and-rubber peak.

This is Lookout Mountain Youth Services Center, the only high-security prison for juveniles in Colorado. More than two hundred boys, ages twelve to eighteen, here for a wide range of offenses, live in campuslike cottages and dorms on the grounds behind a high fence. They attend classes where they can earn a real high school diploma, not a GED, plus take some college-level courses and get treatment and counseling for addiction problems.

Prison Converts to Camp

For two weeks last August, the Lookout Mountain facility was converted into an Angel Tree camp as the Colorado office of

Straight Ahead Ministries brought camping inside the fence. Straight Ahead is a Massachusetts-based evangelical ministry to juvenile offenders.

Since many of the youthful offenders have a parent, usually their father, in prison, these are true Angel Tree children who are already headed down the wrong road. And a few of the boys are fathers themselves. Most of them will serve their term at Lookout Mountain and then be returned to the community. Along with dedicated facility staff, Straight Ahead Colorado director Howard Waller is concerned how they will do when their time behind bars is over.

A former prisoner himself, Waller got the idea of taking the summer camping experience inside a prison to minister to the incarcerated Angel Tree children. In past years, as a Prison Fellowship staffer, Waller had created the first Angel Tree camp with a wilderness-adventure program and the first whitewater-rafting experience for Angel Tree children.

Waller, fifty-seven, now codirects the Colorado office of Straight Ahead Ministries with his wife, Connie. For the Lookout Mountain project, Howard and Connie created a three-part event.

First, three staff members and ten inmates selected by the staff on the basis of program accomplishments left the facility to participate in a five-day overnight wilderness program at Redcloud Camp, a Christian adventure facility located in the San Juan range of the Rocky Mountains. The young men and their adult counselors hiked more than twelve miles through the rugged wilderness. They slept one night on a cliff ledge under the stars at an elevation of more than two miles. "I thought about running," confided one of the boys. "But I was having too much fun."

Next came a five-day program that ran for six hours each afternoon and evening after the residents completed their daily classes and counseling. Waller and his volunteers from Straight Ahead and Bear Valley Church, where Waller serves as the associate pastor for prison ministry, brought in a portable obstacle course, the rock-climb mountain, horse riding and roping, first aid instruction, basketball skills, crafts, compass and navigational training, team-building exercises, a bucking mechanical bull, and survival-skill instruction.

For five days, Straight Ahead replaced the youthful participants' usual prison dinner with home cooking by volunteers and meals donated by local restaurants, including Mexican and Italian food, fried chicken, pizza, and doughnuts.

In the evening, the residents were entertained by a band called Liquid Frequency, keyboard player Michael Lion, and an Elvis impersonator. The evening programs concluded with appearances, autographs, and talks by former professional athletes, including NHL defenseman Dave Feamster of the Chicago Blackhawks, NFL defensive back for the Chicago Bears Mike Spivey, and Dave Stalls, who won a Super Bowl ring with the Oakland Raiders. Howard Waller's son, Randy, who once worked the professional rodeo circuit, flew in from Texas to demonstrate roping and horsemanship. And Jim Walters, a former fighter pilot turned pastor, shared his testimony about high-flying Christian courage with the participants.

The third portion of the project came on Saturday when the entire prison population was invited to participate in a daylong event. The young residents took delight in sending their staff members, including Program Director Bob

Coulson, into the dunking tank. The mechanical bull ride especially challenged these mostly city-raised youth.

End to Match Any End

A music event closed the two-week event, with 160 youth and staff joining hands to sing praise to God. Thirty-one youth took a step forward for Christ. Howard Waller noted that tears streamed down the face of one of the participating staff members. Waller says, "It was an end to match any end. And yet it is not an end, but a great beginning of openness for the youthful residents, their staff, and our volunteers. Straight Ahead and Angel Tree will continue their relationship here with movie and pizza nights for the residents."

Caren Leaf, director of the Lookout Mountain facility, wrote to the Wallers afterward, "I want to share my thanks and excitement with you. The Saturday program for the inmates was a highlight of my professional career."

One of the young inmates who accepted Christ during the week said, "Your programs have given me a chance to have more interaction and team building with the other boys here. Every day, you have something new. I have learned a lot of teamwork and social skills that will help me when I am released next year. I know that all of your people go out of their way to do these things for us, and I really appreciate it. And I'm sure the others do as well."

$\mathcal{U}$-Turn on a Dead-End Road

2002

Life-changing events can take years.

Or a split second.

For Joe Avila, fifty-one, the world turned upside down in one horrifying moment in September 1992—pierced with the sounds of screeching tires, crunching metal, shattered glass, and the last gasps of life.

In the words of his neighbors, Joe was a "good family man"—living in Fresno, California, with his wife, Mary, and daughters Elizabeth and Grace. He made a good living as a site acquisition engineer with Nextel and McCaw Communications. He helped out his neighbors and the community, using his pickup truck to deliver supplies to the homeless shelter and to carry games to church and school carnival fundraisers.

But Joe Avila had a dark side: He was an alcoholic—a dangerous one, with five drunk-driving convictions.

Then, on September 18, 1992, while racing drunkenly down a Fresno freeway, Joe plowed his pickup truck into the rear of a car driven by a seventeen-year-old high school honor student and cheerleader named Amy. The crash killed Amy and severely injured her classmate passenger. Joe fled the scene but was arrested a few hours later at his home.

Five days later, sitting with the chaplain in the Fresno County Jail, a deeply sobered and remorseful Joe gave his life to Christ and asked God to redeem him from his life of sin and alcoholism.

With his prior conviction record and a manslaughter charge, Joe was looking at twelve years in prison. But his attorneys wanted to fight the case. "Everybody does it, we'll get you off," they told him. So Joe put up bail and checked into the Salvation Army Adult Rehabilitation Center while awaiting trial. "I was a brand-new Christian; I needed to get grounded in my faith," he explains. "I started reading the Bible and learning about Christ, especially the forgiving Christ, because that was what I needed most at the time."

When his trial date arrived, the new Joe-in-Christ shocked his attorneys, ordering them to switch his plea to "guilty." No plea-bargaining, no drawn-out trial to punish his family and the victim's family; just prepare for the maximum.

And that's what the judge gave him, twelve years behind bars. "You are an alcoholic," said the judge. "You crave alcohol. There is nothing this court can do to replace [the victim]. There's going to be an emptiness in the lives of her family and friends. Her death is an outrage."

Joe knew that was true, but he also knew that he had, at last, rounded a corner in his life. By accepting responsibility for the terrible thing he had done, he turned away from his "life of lies."

Just before his transfer to the California Men's Colony at San Luis Obispo, Joe's wife, Mary, also accepted Christ as her Savior. Then, together, the couple invited Christ into their marriage.

Joe pledged to make his prison time a learning experience. He started taking classes and studied the Bible nearly every waking moment outside his prison work schedule.

That first fall, when his two daughters visited him in the maximum-security prison, they clearly saw the change in their father. "Dad, we want what you have and what Mom has," they said. So there in the prison visiting room, Joe led Elizabeth and Grace to Christ.

His daughters weren't the only ones to notice the change in Joe's life. He worked in the prison hospital and visited the dying men in the hospice unit. "God gave me the privilege to represent his Son to the dying, the downhearted, and the diseased. I remembered how Jesus embraced the lepers, and I tried to be like him in embracing men dying of AIDS or cancer."

Meanwhile, on the outside, Mary waited. "We knew that prison can tear a marriage up," says Joe. "We decided that we would use phone calls only for a quick hello, prayer, or to talk with the children. When major issues had to be discussed, they were taken up by letter or during in-person visits."

Just before Joe's first Christmas behind bars, he heard about Prison Fellowship's Angel Tree and signed his daughters up to receive gifts. A volunteer at the PF Fresno office took the application and made the delivery. When Joe heard his girls' "Thank you, Daddy" over the phone, he said, "Thank you, God."

Then Joe discovered *Inside Journal,* PF's newspaper for prisoners. He began reading it and sharing it with his family. Though Joe's daughters, then fourteen and eight, were receiving Angel Tree gifts themselves, they used their limited family funds to buy gifts for other Angel Tree children. Grace, the youngest, wrote a letter to the imprisoned father of the girl she bought gifts for, and eventually the letter was published in

Inside Journal. Other prisoners at the facility read the letter in the paper and sought out Joe for his testimony.

Joe returned home from prison on January 6, 1999, paroled after serving six and a half years. Joe joined the PF staff on January 6, 2000.

Joe has made a sharp U-turn in life since that day nine years ago when he took an innocent life. He has candidly told his story to hundreds of others—to prisoners, to community and church groups, to kids who get drunk. And although it never gets easier for him to admit to others that he killed someone, he continues to do it. "The greatest thing I can do to honor Amy," he says, "is to live the life I'm living now"—as a new man, redeemed by God's grace. "I won't sway from that."

Sharing God's Love Through Angel Tree

The Testimonies of Elizabeth and Grace Avila

2002

Joe Avila's daughters, Elizabeth and Grace, were six and ten years old when he went away to prison for almost seven years. Today Elizabeth is in college, and Grace is in high school. At a recent Angel Tree event, they spoke about why Angel Tree means so much to them.

Elizabeth: "One of the hardest things was that we were such a close family. I was about to turn eleven. And through high school and junior high, I was a cheerleader, so Dad missed my cheerleading at games and competitions. And my first date.

"It was hardest around birthdays and holidays and especially Christmas. When he wasn't there it was hard, especially for my mom."

Grace: "I was so young when my dad was away. In my elementary years, he missed my school functions and my soccer games. What made it especially hard was when I would see my friends with their fathers—most of them had fathers—at the soccer games and the practices.

"And Christmas was very hard, because every Christmas we went to church together for a special dinner. When Angel Tree began, it was so much better because you'd get a gift."

Elizabeth: "We had the Angel Tree process explained to us beforehand. We knew what was coming, because my dad told us that we'd all be getting a gift for Christmas. But over the years we received them several different ways. We'd go to parties at the church, which was fun, but some of the best times were when someone personally delivered the gifts. Not only would we see the love from our dad, but we'd see the love from someone we didn't know—a complete stranger. I felt completely unforgotten. People remembered."

Grace: "I remember one Christmas when about six volunteers came over. I was with my friends—they all knew about my dad and where he was. And my friends were surprised to see me get these gifts from him. We had this big party, and my mom made apple cider ... it was just a fun time. And it wouldn't have happened without Angel Tree. I'm very thankful."

"Our church was very involved in Angel Tree and with Prison Fellowship. At one Christmas several years before he came home, when they asked people to come up and take an angel off the tree, I remembered the joy that I had when I received gifts. So I wanted to do anything that was possible for any other child with a parent in prison to receive that joy."

Elizabeth: "Soon after we started receiving Christmas gifts, we decided with our mom that we wanted to give to other kids as well as receive. Last year was probably one of our most memorable Christmases. Janelle, one of the coordinators in the Fresno area, was delivering gifts in a city named Avenal, which is about sixty miles from Fresno. She showed up at one of the houses and knocked on the door. A little boy named Brian, who was in fifth grade, answered it and told her that his mom was at work and he had two younger brothers who were with baby-sitters. When Janelle walked in, she noticed that it was a tiny house, and there was no furniture and no curtains. There was just a small kitchen table with one chair in the kitchen; there was nowhere to sit in the living room; just a blank room with one small TV. There was a small Christmas tree that Brian had decorated with paper ornaments. When Janelle saw all of this, she realized how much more in need they were.

"She told Brian that the gifts were from his father, who was in prison in Southern California, and that they were given to him through the love of Jesus.

"The next day Janelle called our dad (he's now the Prison Fellowship director in Fresno) and said there is so much more that we can do for this family—that they are in a lot of need.

"Janelle worked at a furniture store where they took used furniture in trade. We got a truck and loaded a bunch of furniture on it and then bought a lot of food and more presents for the children. On Christmas morning we got up about 5:00 A.M. and drove to Avenal. When we knocked on the door, the mother answered. She was in shock! She was so happy, and surprised. She spoke little English, mostly Spanish. We went inside and put curtains up and gave them the food and furniture.

"We explained to them that this was through the love of Jesus, and that we got to know them through Angel Tree because their father filled out the application. We explained to her a little about Jesus—my dad can speak Spanish—and she looked at us as we told her about how our own father had been in prison. Then we all prayed and she accepted the Lord.

"Then Brian said he wanted the same thing, that he understood what was going on, and he wanted Jesus for himself. So he also accepted Jesus. Now they go to church near their home, and my dad stops by every once in a while and drops off books and little surprises."

$\mathcal{W}$HEN HOPE WHEELS IN

1994

"Dear Angel Tree ... I am [in] a very hard situation, but I think that my family is in a worse one."

So began a letter from Arizona prisoner Ramon, asking for a Christmas gift for his four-year-old son. But his request bypassed the typical talk of toys or clothing. "I am begging for your help to get a wheelchair—any kind of wheelchair," he pleaded. "It is to move my son to any place he has to go."

Since infancy and a bout with meningitis, the child had been paralyzed; his mother carried him from place to place. Trying to care for four young children in an impoverished section of Nogales, she did all she could to "bring food to the house," Ramon wrote. But sometimes the meager funds earned from sewing, ironing, or selling homemade tortillas didn't cover the costs of both food and the boy's medicine.

Local Prison Fellowship staff sent the letter to Christ Community Church in Tucson, where a group of ten couples raised the money to buy a customized pediatric wheelchair. They also collected and delivered three huge bags of food, clothes for all four children—including winter coats—toys, toiletries, blankets, and towels.

Christ Community's ministry has extended beyond Christmas. A physician who travels weekly to Nogales has offered to treat the inmate's family free of charge; other church members are investigating channels to get the boy into therapy and special educational programs.

Church member Melanie Semler explains they want to do everything they can to help, "because this is a ministry to a father's children"—done on his behalf. "And if *my* husband were gone," she adds, "I'd hope that someone would do something like this for me."

$\mathcal{W}$HY SHE VOLUNTEERS

1997

Annette Pike, Angel Tree coordinator in Portland, Oregon, was just over a year old when her father left to begin his criminal career. She couldn't remember him, and the few times she asked about him, her mother gave only curt answers. At five she gained a stepfather when her mother remarried.

"But there was always a part of me that wondered what my real father was like," Annette says. "Something was missing."

In fifth grade, Annette asked about him again, and this time her mother pulled out a stash of birthday and Christmas cards—all from her father, sent during his ten years in prison. All intercepted by her mom.

Annette wept as she read them. "He had written notes that he loved me, that he wished he could be there, that he hoped I had a good Christmas or birthday. I was so happy and so angry: Why didn't she give them to me before?"

Surprisingly, her dad telephoned the following day: Now out of prison, he wanted to come see her. A week later the two went shopping, and her dad offered to buy her anything she wanted. Annette picked out a simple cream-colored sweater—which she wore repeatedly and has kept to this day. "I'll always cherish that sweater," she says, "because he gave it to me in love."

Afterward they started writing, "and it made me so happy to be able to express my love to him," she recalls. Sadly, her father died less than two years later.

Today, Annette champions the ministry of Angel Tree, "because I think the gifts represent the love their parents have for them, even though the parents made some ugly mistakes. If I could have had contact with my father as a child, maybe some healing would have come sooner. I lost out on the love of my father."

$\mathscr{A}$DAM REMEMBERS ANGEL TREE

2003

When Donna Scott married an Oregon prisoner after seven months of letter writing, five-year-old Adam looked forward to visiting his new stepfather every Saturday. Their time together was limited but "awesome," Adam describes, recalling the children's playroom in the prison's visiting area—where he and stepdad Josh could watch videos, play dodge ball, and eat junk food from the vending machine.

"I really didn't think of it as going to prison," adds Adam. "I thought of it as going to see my dad!"

Since his mom and biological father had divorced when Adam was three, "I never really got a chance to let him into my heart," he explains. "But Josh, I really did love *him* in my heart. I felt he was my number-one father."

Their relationship grew strong and comfortable during seven years of weekend visits to the prison, augmented by regular phone calls and letters. When Adam started receiving Christmas presents through Angel Tree, "those were the gifts I looked forward to the most," he remembers. "They were from *Dad*—and were things that I wanted!" Like a big box of paints and crayons "because I loved to doodle." And twenty-five packs of football cards at a time when collecting and trading sports cards was a favorite hobby.

What's more, those Angel Tree gifts allowed the youngster "one of the few times during the whole school year that I could connect with the other kids," he says. "After Christmas, they'd all say, 'Look at what my dad got me.' And *I* could say the same thing."

Loss of Trust

Sadly, the family life that seemed so promising on the inside quickly withered after Josh's 1991 release. Nine years of prison's regimented confines left him sorely unprepared to take responsibility for himself and a full-time family, especially a son just entering his teenage years. "In January, you had to tell Josh what to do; he wasn't used to making any decisions whatsoever," recalls Donna. "In February you could give him two choices and he'd pick one. By March he was just starting to relax and feel more comfortable about going out in the world. Then April came and a buddy of his got out of prison, too—and that was it. Josh spent practically all day and all night at his house. During the summer, Adam and I were like a single-parent family again."

Even so, Adam says, "I never thought he would leave us."

But only nine months out of prison, that's just what Josh did—ostensibly for an out-of-state job. A few months later he returned—with a new girlfriend and divorce papers for Donna.

"That's when the feelings started kicking in," says Adam—battering feelings of betrayal, abandonment, rage ... and guilt. "Adam was the one who opened the door when Josh came and served me with the papers," Donna remembers. "He felt if he hadn't opened the door, the divorce wouldn't have happened."

But most of all, says Adam, "what hurt is that I let this guy into my heart as my father, and he just turned around and left me. It seemed like all those years visiting in prison, all those promises he made, were just a waste of my life."

And Josh's exodus soured more than one relationship: "He also took away the trust I'd had in anyone else," explains Adam. At thirteen, he withdrew from friends, spending hours alone in his room, where "no one else could hurt me."

The one relationship that endured and deepened during the subsequent years was the one between mother and son. "We really learned to talk things out," says Donna. No concern, no question, no feeling was off-limits for sharing.

Donna also became close to the Oregon Prison Fellowship staff, "who supported me wholeheartedly," she says. That relationship started while Josh was still incarcerated and helped the family through the tough trials of separation by prison as well as separation by desertion.

"It's like swimming," Donna illustrates. "You can't breathe because you're underwater for so long and you've got to get that air. So you're swimming up to the top as fast as you can until you break through the surface of the water and suck in that big gulp of air. And then you can start breathing again. That's Prison Fellowship; that's my gulp of air.

"I don't even want to think about where I would have been without them," she adds. "Both Adam and I would have been cut off from the world."

Indeed, Linda Leahy, then PF Oregon's office coordinator, taught Donna how to drive—from *scratch*, unbeknownst to Linda at the time. "We were heading onto the freeway," recalls Linda with a smile, "and I asked her how much time she had practiced driving. She looked at the clock and said, 'About twenty minutes!'"

Donna also started volunteering in the PF office, sometimes taking Adam with her to help. One day as they stuffed envelopes, the famished boy pleaded for a lunch break. "Pretty soon," Donna promised. Then Adam asked, "Where are all these letters going?"

"To churches," Mom answered, "to tell them about Angel Tree."

Suddenly Adam stuffed faster and faster—eager, or so his mother thought, to just get through the job and be off to lunch. "Slow down," she prodded. "We'll make it to McDonald's."

"You don't understand, Mom," Adam corrected. "The more envelopes we get stuffed, the more kids who will get presents from their dads!"

Not Left Alone

Though once-promising bonds between Adam and his step-dad painfully split apart, Adam still praises Angel Tree for helping him feel valued and more connected with other kids at school, whose dads were more involved in their lives. He encourages churches to take an ongoing interest in prisoners' children, beyond the Christmas program. "It's good to have people to talk to in tough situations," he says. "If you don't have anyone to talk to, you're pretty much by yourself." Again, he locks on to his own memories of isolation and pain. "I would want to reassure them"—other prisoners' kids—"that just because your dad left you, it doesn't mean every single other person is going to leave you. That's one thing I would let them know."

Both Adam and Donna have learned, too, that no matter how many others may turn away, God will never abandon them. "When Josh left is when I started going to church consistently, going to Bible studies, having fellowship with other Christians, and gaining a better relationship with God," says Donna.

Today, Adam is twenty-three and works three jobs while completing college. Though he no longer lives at home, "our communication is better than ever," says Mom.

Donna, who went back to college in her thirties ("Some of my fellow students hadn't even been born the last time I was in school!"), now teaches middle-school math in Heppner, Oregon, a small town of about 1,500 people. "No stoplights—just stop *signs*," she describes. "One gas station, a grocery store, but no fast food chains. The Department of Motor Vehicles is open only one day a week, and there's no mail delivery. Everyone has a P.O. box." And it's so *quiet*, Donna adds—a far cry from the cacophony of thundering semi-trucks, wailing sirens, and screeching tires she'd gotten used to in the city. "I can go sit in the backyard and just think."

Sometimes she thinks about where she's been and where she's headed. "All those years of knowing the Lord," she reflects, "I would turn my life over to him but I'd still want to hold on to a piece of it. Now I give my future to him with no strings."

She's just as fervently committed to Angel Tree—and thrilled that the pastor of her new church, Willow Creek Baptist, wants to minister to prisoners' children year-round, not simply at Christmas. "That's where my heart is, too," she says. Because she knows from experience that the healing of some wounds takes more time.

Part V

Reaching Prisoners and Parents

There's power in a gift. Our mighty God has used this gift-giving ministry to penetrate prison walls and soften hardened hearts, to transform the spirits and minds of prisoner- and free-world parents.

$\mathcal{T}$HERE'S POWER IN A GIFT

by Howard Waller

1998

I first noted Joe Turley's name in 1994, when I joined Prison Fellowship staff as director for Angel Tree in Colorado. Every two months Angel Tree received a money order from an inmate at Limon, a maximum-security facility. I knew the money order represented about 50 percent of a prisoner's paltry wages. Who was this guy—Joe Turley? We had no record of his attending any of our many PF programs. So, early in 1996, I went to Limon and asked if I could meet him.

Murder in His Eyes
The officer in charge scowled. "Turley?" He was one of the roughest inmates in the system. Even some of the officers kept their distance. Was I sure I wanted to meet him?

Waiting alone in the visiting area, I prayed for wisdom—and courage—which I almost lost when Joe walked in. He looked like an outlaw. Unshaven. Wide, rigid, angry shoulders. I reached to shake his hand; he kept his hands to himself. "What do you want?" he blurted.

I explained my curiosity about the money orders.

"Look, the only reason I am talking to you is because they said you are an ex-con." *As if that earned me some respect.* "I am the worst of the worst. I'm in here for three life sentences without possibility of parole, for killing three people." *As if I'd better respect him.*

I asked again about the Angel Tree money. He said, "About six years ago, I filled out one of those forms. I thought it was probably a con, but what did I have to lose? Then after Christmas I saw my son—his once-a-year visit. He came up to me and shouted thanks for the gifts I sent him at Christmas.... Since then, I have always given to that Angel Tree, and I always will."

So he wouldn't notice my tears, I pretended to sneeze. "Joe, this year let us take your boy to summer camp." Josh was ten, the perfect age for our one-week program at Redcloud Christian Camp.

"Waller, I don't have the money to send him to camp, and I won't owe nobody."

I explained that local churches give camp scholarships to Angel Tree kids, but he wouldn't hear of it. The conversation would have been over if I hadn't thought quickly: "I hear you work in the leather shop. Make me something of the value of the camp, and we'll be even."

Joe could live with that, though there seemed to be murder in his eyes when I mentioned Jesus. "Have you ever invited Christ into your life?" I asked. He stormed toward the door. He could walk away from me. It would be harder for him to walk away from God.

A Child Chinks the Wall
Over the next months, every time I went to Limon, I would track down Joe. And in July I saw Josh off to Redcloud, a

mountain camp that challenges kids physically. It has a ropes course, canoeing, horseback riding. Redcloud also challenges kids spiritually, especially through an invitation of commitment to Christ at a closing campfire.

My wife, Connie, and I "took" to Josh—the center of attention, the first to rappel down the rocks. As likable as he was, he had his own means of keeping people at arm's length, as if his laughter and zealous energy were defensive weapons. Like his father's anger, just more subtle.

Soon after that camp, I received a package from Limon. I gasped when I saw Joe's exquisite leather work. I was eager to thank him a few weeks later when I would be at Limon for a PF evangelistic "yard event" featuring a crowd-drawing athlete as speaker.

Joe found me before I found him. Greeting the inmates, I felt someone nudge my elbow. It was Joe. I sensed the other men dropping back, giving space. Joe's voice was stern: "Josh has changed."

"What do you mean?" I stammered, thinking something horrible had happened.

"He found that Christ of yours."

We didn't have much time to talk that day, but he introduced me to his brother as "Waller, the guy who took Josh to camp." He showed me photos of Josh and him—BP, before prison.

After that I visited Joe about once a month. In November he sent a package of handmade leather gloves and intricately beaded barrettes—for Angel Tree children. And in December, standing in the chapel door at the Limon Christmas service, I felt an elbow in my ribs.

"Howard," he said (this was a switch; he always called me Waller), "I found a new relationship with Jesus." With that he squeezed my shoulder with a vice grip. I tried not to notice the tear in his eye, but there was no mistaking his smile.

God had broken through. How? Through the witness of a child who had accepted Christ at an Angel Tree camp. Through correspondence, Josh had told Joe about his trust in God, his freer spirit, his new church home. He'd sent Joe to the Bible, looking for some answers.

Joe sensed a respectable difference in Josh, and so have I. One example: Last year, camp-bound, Josh did *not* want to ride in the same van as his older stepbrother. A year later at Redcloud I saw the two hanging out together. "We're 'buds' now," Josh confided, acknowledging that walls have come down.

And I see a marked difference in father Joe. His "fortress" is no longer defined by anger. He carries himself with a new demeanor because he has a new source of strength. I see other prisoners having a new respect for him. This year he's drawing other craftsmen into his vision to design and make gloves, jewelry, and scarves for Angel Tree kids.

I have searched our files to identify what church sent that first Angel Tree gift to the child of a man self-described as "the worst of the worst." I can't track them down. So here, on behalf of Joe and every prisoner separated from his or her child, I thank all Angel Tree volunteers and donors.

The government says Joe has "no possibility" of parole. But by God's grace a redeemed Joe has every possibility of abundant life. That's because there's power in the Gift.

Postscript

After reading Joe Turley's story in an Angel Tree newsletter, prisoners at the Federal Correctional Institution in Englewood, Colorado, determined to find a way to raise funds to send Joshua to camp. Word spread throughout the compound that inmates were helping the child of another inmate, and funds from modestly paid prisoner employment flowed in. The prisoners raised enough cash to send Joshua and six other Angel Tree children to camp for a week.

"I am writing to express my thanks for your faithfulness to our heavenly Father and to my daughter and me over the past five years that I have been locked up. You have made sure that my daughter received something from me and for her to know that I love her and she is in my heart and on my mind.

"For this next Christmas season I have a request, just once: Could you please have a photo sent to me of my daughter receiving her gift? I would like to see the expression on her face as she is receiving or opening the gift. Thank you."

—Prisoner-dad

$\mathcal{T}$IME OUT TO KNOW GOD

2003

One quiet Sunday evening in March 1994, Pat Nolan pulled his five- and six-year-old daughters close to him in their living room. He had thought long and hard about how to word his announcement, so they could understand what was happening without being afraid.

"Courtney, Katie," he began gently. "Has someone ever told the teacher that you did something that you didn't do, and you got a time-out?" Both girls nodded. They understood this level of injustice and punishment.

"Well, some people told some lies about Daddy, and *I'm* getting a time-out," Pat continued. He inhaled a deep breath, as if trying to suck in extra courage. "I have to go to a prison camp, and I'll have to be away from home for a long time."

Katie, the younger child, perked up at the familiar mention of *camp*. "Will you take a sleeping bag and sleep in a tent?" she asked innocently. Courtney's furrowed brow signaled confusion. *Daddy's going away?*

The next day Pat and a friend of his drove to Dublin, California, about eighty-five miles from the Nolans' Elk Grove home outside Sacramento. For Pat, it was a one-way trip; he now belonged to the Federal Bureau of Prisons.

Investigations and Allegations

Just weeks earlier, the fifteen-year California assemblyman had pleaded guilty to one count of racketeering. It came as a shock to those who knew Pat but not the circumstances. To both constituents and colleagues, the Catholic conservative was known as "a straight arrow," a law-and-order guy, "a pudgy Eagle Scout"— as one reporter had described him. But nearly six years earlier, FBI agents had swarmed his office—unannounced and while Pat was gone—and spent the next five hours rifling through file cabinets and desk drawers. That day launched a prolonged and virulent investigation, targeting other legislators as well as Pat, to root out alleged "corruption in the Capitol"—such as trading votes on bills for lobbyists' lucrative contributions. Anyone socially or professionally connected to Pat could be grilled— and regrilled—for hours at a time.

Throughout most of the ordeal, Pat clung to the belief that truth would triumph. The first year or so, "I kept expecting to get a phone call saying it had all been a big mistake, that I was exonerated." But the call never came. As he and Gail started and added to their family, the stigma of suspicion and the threat of an ugly court battle shrouded them in a chilling fog.

Finally, when a trial was certain, Pat's attorney laid it on the line: "You have a strong case, and I can put on a strong defense," he told Pat and Gail. But the government had charged Pat with six counts of wrongdoing. Conviction on any *one* of those counts would mean a minimum of more than eight years in prison.

The government had made an offer: twenty-two months in prison in return for a one-count guilty plea and Pat's implication of other legislators. With*out* his testimony, thirty-three months.

Pat immediately refused to be manipulated into testifying against anyone else. But the option of a plea bargain presented the most difficult struggle of his life. "My reputation for integrity was the hallmark of my public service," he explains. "Should I plead guilty to a crime I did not commit?"—which would shatter his reputation and his career, but ensure a shorter separation from his family. "Or should I fight for my good name" in a hostile, highly publicized trial, with the risk of losing his freedom and his family for many more years?

But as he grappled with his options, only one made sense. "Gail and the children were the most important things in my life by far," affirms Pat. "I wasn't willing to risk losing them."

God in the Loneliness

Pat arrived at the prison with a few extra clothes, his Bible, and a determination to find some good in this ordeal. A friend had encouraged him to make his prison time a "monastic experience"—a time to grow closer to God, who had a purpose in all that was happening.

But even under the watchful eye of God, Pat slept little that first night, amid the nonstop din of fifty other "dorm mates" who snored, shifted noisily in their bunks, and shambled to the bathroom at all hours. "But that's not all that kept me awake," he remembers. "I missed Gail and the children."

Just that morning, on his way to prison, he had dropped Courtney off at kindergarten. In her life one moment; out of it the next. "Children that age don't understand the legal issues," he says now. "All they understand is that you're not there for them. They feel abandoned. And that hurts."

For several weeks, in fact, delayed paperwork prevented Pat

country. Justice Fellowship—based outside of Washington, D.C.—was looking for a new president. Would Pat be interested in interviewing for the job?

So less than two months after walking out of prison, Pat assumed his new position.

As the ministry's key advocate of restorative justice, Pat not surprisingly champions the restorative nature of Angel Tree. He seizes every opportunity to tell others how the program allowed a helpless, absent father send a special delivery of love to his children at Christmas.

"The body of Christ visited me in prison; the body of Christ welcomed my children," he says, once again stopping to dab tears from his eyes. Consequently, "I went into prison believing in God, but I came out *knowing* him."

But Pat doesn't just *talk* about Angel Tree; each Christmas the whole Nolan family purchases and delivers gifts to local prisoners' kids. "It's not just to give back for what *they* received through Angel Tree," says Pat. "But it's also to help my children see the power of the gospel and the love of Jesus Christ."

Son Jamie has seen that transforming love. A few years ago his Sunday school teacher assigned the class to make pictures of someplace they would find Jesus. Using crayons, glue, and popsicle sticks, most of the six-year-olds made a church or a house. Jamie made a jail.

The other kids laughed at him. "Why would you make *that?*" his teacher asked.

"Because my dad goes to jail," Jamie answered confidently, "and he tells the guys that Jesus loves them. And he teaches them not to steal anymore."

"You can't say it any more clearly than that," says Pat with a burst of fatherly pride. "He's seen that even in pain, there can be joy." The joy of God's presence—even during a time-out behind bars.

$\mathcal{A}$ Blessing Returned

2001

In 1998 Tom and Tricia Irwin of Hempstead, Texas, noticed a table sign at their church seeking volunteers for Prison Fellowship's Angel Tree program.

They signed up, took tags for two children from one family, and purchased the suggested gifts. On a Saturday just before Christmas, they delivered the gifts to the home, gratified by touching the lives of two little boys.

Later, Tom wrote a short note to the children's father, Richard, who was serving time in a federal prison in Tennessee. To his surprise, he received a response. As the months passed, Tom and Richard exchanged many letters, though the inmate struggled with his writing skills. Tom learned that Richard had grown up in the Hempstead area and had become a major drug dealer. Even though he was now serving twenty-five years in prison, Richard believed God had turned around a bad situation for his good purpose—to bring Richard to Christ. He became a Christian five months after arriving in prison. In every letter to Tom, he was full of praise for his Savior, Jesus.

After a year and a half of letters, Richard wrote that he was being transferred to a minimum-security facility at Beaumont, about an hour from Houston. He asked if Tom would visit him.

Tom knew nothing about prisons or prisoners and was apprehensive. But he agreed to visit Richard. Waiting in the visiting room, Tom wondered if the attitude of the real person would match the encouraging words of his letters. And then Richard appeared, a smile on his face and obvious peace in his heart. "As we talked I could see how Jesus had changed his life," Tom observed.

"Here was a man who could barely write a simple sentence, and I remembered how the Jewish leaders had marveled at Peter and John as uneducated and untrained men who had 'been with Jesus.' Richard—who had had some bad breaks in life and made some bad choices—was someone who had 'been with Jesus.' And where I had gone to bless him, he was now blessing me!"

To Hannah With Love

2001

Three weeks before Hannah was born, her mother, Christina, came home to find her apartment surrounded by police cars. Hannah's father, Scott, had violated probation and was headed for the county jail.

"It was so hard," Christina says. "I was eight and a half months pregnant when Scott got locked up! But when Hannah was born my parents were there, Scott's parents were there ... and I was on the phone with Scott the entire time. He kept calling in from jail!"

In the year that followed, Christina and Scott were married by proxy on March 30, 2001. Christina, with little Hannah along, drove every weekend to visit Scott—but their no-contact visitations were hard to bear. Scott never got a chance to hold his baby girl or kiss his young bride. And when Hannah's first birthday came around in October, there was nothing he could do to show her that he loved her.

Enter Angel Tree ...

"What your ministry did for my daughter has touched my heart in a way no one else ever has," Christina wrote the day after Christmas. "I was gearing up for another heart-wrenching Christmas without my husband and then, after one very hectic day, I came home to find a trash bag tied to my door. At first I thought I had the wrong apartment, then I thought someone had played a joke on us. But when I opened that bag and found presents that said 'Daddy loves you. Happy holidays,' I just broke down and cried.

"I was never expecting in my wildest dreams that someone would reach out to my family and my daughter like that," she continues. "My husband had not told me about Angel Tree, so the surprise was absolutely awesome, and you will never know how much I needed that. You guys really made my Christmas complete, and I know you have filled my husband's heart with joy that he could send some presents to our daughter's first Christmas experience."

It was God's special providence that the church wasn't able to deliver the gifts personally to Christina. Because the gifts were left like a package at her door, it made her feel that her husband himself had sent the gifts—a special need for a young newlywed.

Hannah gleefully tore through the wrapping paper—opening boxes containing two tiny outfits and an inflatable "Blues Clues" chair. "It plays music when you press a button," Christina says. "She goes over to it and presses that button over and over each day!

"Being able to give us something for her first real Christmas made Scott feel really good," Christina adds. "It really hurts him not to be able to get her stuff, and Angel Tree really meant so much. I even saved the gift tags and wrote the story in Hannah's baby book so that she won't forget how much her daddy loved her, even when he was away."

Hannah is walking now ... and getting into a lot of trouble.

She loves to have her mom read her books almost as much as she loves getting into the cabinets at their apartment. She's beginning to be able to communicate with her dad now, too. When Hannah comes to visit, they both stick out their tongues at each other through the glass.

"I have a really great job at the Church of Glad Tidings," Christina says. "I work in their day care so I can be with my daughter every day. I've even started attending services with them every Sunday morning.

"Thank you for truly filling my heart with the love of Jesus and for your endless mission to seek and save the lost. Your work is not in vain, and may God bless you in everything you do!"

"I want to tell you how the Lord has blessed my family through the Angel Tree ministry. I see, on a daily basis, the havoc wrought by sinful actions of others on the lives of innocent children. I am a homicide detective. My support of your ministry has allowed me to help share the gospel with the families of people I have dealt with on a professional basis, and with some of those people whom I have sent to jail or prison. But I never considered how your ministry might touch my own family. I have a brother-in-law and a nephew—both have children—who are in prison. On Christmas Day I was told by their families that their children had been blessed by Angel Tree for the past two years and that my grandniece's favorite music tape is by Steven Curtis Chapman, which she received through Angel Tree. These children live in a different state, so Angel Tree is the only personal Christian influence in their lives. My nephew sent word to my wife and me that he wants us to send him an easily understood translation of the Bible, as the only translation available to him is difficult to read. This is from a young man who did not read before prison. He says he is studying Scripture on a regular basis through one of your Bible studies. When I was told this, I couldn't help crying tears of praise for God's faithfulness. Thank you for your faithfulness in proclaiming the Word and thank you for showing Christ's love to 'the least of these.'"

—*Angel Tree donor*

$\mathcal{A}$ Springtime of Grace

by Spring D.

1999

Angel Tree was important to our family because the results lasted long past the Christmas season. In 1990 my husband, Mike, went to prison. That was hard for me to handle. I even attempted suicide, but I know now that God had other plans.

We have a daughter and a son, who were eight and six years old then. As Christmas approached, I knew it was going to be hard. It wasn't just that finances were tight; Daddy wouldn't be home like he had been before. The holidays would not be happy.

The chaplain at the prison encouraged Mike to sign up for Angel Tree, and he did. As Christmas approached, I got a call from a woman named Kelly, from Faith Bible Alliance Church in nearby Neosho, Iowa. She said she had some Christmas gifts for us from Mike, and some food for the family, and arranged to come to our home to drop them off.

When Kelly came, she was so friendly you would have thought she had known me for years. She was eight months pregnant at that time and had to have help carrying everything.

The kids were amazed at the gifts because they were old enough to know their daddy was in prison. They asked how he was able to get out to go shopping. I explained that some

Christians wanted to help and had done the shopping for him. It impressed the kids to know that people who didn't even know us cared that much. Some other people we had known had pretty much turned their backs on us when Mike went to prison.

I had not been active in any church for some time. I had gone to a couple of Bible studies, but just wasn't sure where I stood. After Kelly delivered the gifts, she called us at least once a week. She was persistent!

And it wasn't just talk. Her whole family got involved helping us in practical ways. At one point during the winter, I got an awful cold and was miserable. One evening, who should come to the door but Kelly's husband, Terry, and their sons, with meals for us! Not only that, we were heating by woodburner and they offered to bring in wood for us until I was feeling better.

Mike got out of prison in July 1993, and I decided to have a "welcome home" party for him. I invited some of the couples from the church, since I had begun to attend activities there. He couldn't believe that these Christians who didn't even know him could welcome him so warmly. We started attending church as a family.

But things didn't get easy immediately once Mike got out. We had some financial troubles, and Mike began selling drugs to make money. He was using, too, and soon became his own best customer. In 1994 he was arrested again. This was a big blow, and again I considered suicide.

The church didn't let us down—they continued to be supportive. Pastor Fletcher laid it on the line to both of us. He told me that suicide was not an option, and neither was divorce. He told Mike that he couldn't continue to put his family though this. He was firm but loving. I think what really made the difference in Mike's attitude, though, was when our son asked him, "Daddy, do you love drugs more than you love me?" Mike had to think seriously about that one.

Amazingly enough, Mike's parole officer did not send him back to prison. After three months in the Milwaukee House of Correction, he had to do three months in drug rehabilitation. Given this chance, with the help of the church, we became more involved in activities there. In September 1995 all four of us were baptized and rededicated our lives to the Lord. Kelly's family and many of the church members who had been so active in our Christian growth were there to take part in the occasion.

Our participation in the church continues to grow. It is hard to believe, but Mike was recently made a trustee, and I am a deaconess. We are beginning to get other opportunities to reach out to others, just as others helped us in the past. We know that we need God's help in keeping our relationship strong as we serve the Lord in new ways.

"On July 23,1993, I was sentenced to seven years 'hard time' for several felony convictions after a jury trial. I was taken away from my wife and four children. My boys were seven and two and my twin girls were eight months old. For me, time went by quickly and easily, as long as I didn't think about what my wife had on her plate, and that's all I thought about.

"I came to accept Jesus within days of my incarceration by what I believe was the intervention of an angel. Within days of being incarcerated I was involved in a life-threatening situation which only God could have got me out of, but that's another story.

"When I heard about Angel Tree, I immediately signed up my kids. Just hearing about it and what they do brought tears to my eyes. On that Christmas day of 1993 my family came to visit me in the afternoon. I became filled with joy and totally thankful to Jesus and Angel Tree because of what transpired in the first few minutes of that Christmas afternoon. My boys ran up to me (as they always did) full of excitement because of the presents that God (and I) had given to these two boys. For the next hour all they did was tell me about the gifts they received and wanted to know from me how I knew what they wanted. My twin girls were each carrying a doll from Santa. They looked so fulfilled and content. My wife then went on to tell me everything that the Angel Tree volunteers had done for my family, including a dinner for my wife.

"After my family left I went back to my cell and began to weep very hard and give thanks to the Lord. I made a vow at that time that I would continue to walk with the Lord and never look back. The following year Angel Tree fulfilled the dreams of my children again, and again after they left I began to weep and give thanks to the Lord. On April 21, 1995, my conviction was overturned and I was released. I am still walking with the Lord as I anticipate I always will. My wife and I have continuously donated to Angel Tree and we will continue to do so. Thank you so much."

—*Ex-Prisoner*

The Real Thing

by Mark Hubbell

1994

At one point during a prison seminar, Angel Tree applications were passed out to the men at the Shutter Creek Correctional Institution near Coos Bay, Oregon. A few months later, as the Prison Fellowship area director, I dropped in on one session of another seminar at this prison. Two inmates, previously skeptical and critical of the Angel Tree program, were there, and we visited during a break. I asked if they were still cynical about Christianity. One of them said, "Can I tell you something?" He then went on to tell me that they had decided to prove that Christians were "a bunch of fakes" by filling out and returning Angel Tree applications. They were sure that if they did, they could document the fact that Christians do not really care. I asked them what happened.

The man teared up and said, "Last weekend I got my first visit from my family since I've been moved to this prison. My little boy ran up to me, hugged me, and thanked me for the Tonka truck I'd given him for Christmas. I didn't give him that truck, or the new clothes he was wearing. A church in Springfield, Oregon, had."

Later in that seminar, both men responded to an invitation to receive Christ.

"Yesterday you opened your hearts, arms, and church doors to my precious daughters. You showed them the story of Jesus, gave them presents and said they were from me, and you loved them. You were an answer to my prayers in such a way that I was moved to address my fellow inmates about you this morning in church. I asked my fellow inmates, 'How do we show gratitude to these people who we may never meet?' I suggested that we let God live through us like we see him in them."

—*Prisoner*

How to Get Involved in Angel Tree

Since its beginning in 1982, Angel Tree Christmas has touched millions of children's lives through the loving participation of thousands of churches. And the numbers continue to grow. Each year we receive tens of thousands of Angel Tree applications from prisoners throughout the country, thankful for this opportunity to provide Christmas gifts for their children back home. Currently about two million children have a mom or dad in prison—sometimes both! Angel Tree's goal is to reach every one of these children with the love and touch of Jesus Christ.

How Angel Tree Works

When your church decides to participate in Angel Tree Christmas, Prison Fellowship will send the designated contact person will receive a list of names and contact information of prisoners' children in your local area—as many as your church requests. Volunteers from your church will then contact the children's caregivers to find out what those children want and need. Each child should receive two gifts: one clothing item and one "fun" gift (toys, sports equipment, music CDs, books, etc.).

Next, church volunteers write the children's names and requests on paper angels provided by Prison Fellowship and hang the angels on an Angel Tree in your church. This might be a real or artificial Christmas tree, or another type of display.

Members of your congregation are invited to pick names from the tree and purchase and wrap the requested gifts.

Shortly before Christmas Day, your volunteers will deliver the gifts to the children. Many churches set up "delivery teams" to visit each family's home at a prearranged time that is mutually convenient. Other churches opt to invite all of the prisoners' families to their church for a festive Angel Tree party that includes refreshments and a special program.

Of course, not every child will jump for joy at the sight of his or her gift. Some may not even seem grateful. But they are. Deep down they realize that their mom or dad in prison still loves them and is thinking about them. And over time, that knowledge will usually bear fruit.

Over time, we have seen broken hearts healed and torn families reconciled. A single seed, planted by the simple giving of a gift, can burst into a flourishing harvest under the nurturing hands of God.

Angel Tree: Blessings for Everyone

Yet as much as Angel Tree does to touch the lives of prisoners' children, it can also be a life-changing experience for *you*.

This is a program that everyone in the family can get involved in, from the youngest to the oldest, sowing unforgettable lessons about the real meaning of Christmas and the joy of giving to those in need. Many families, for example, like to purchase and deliver gifts to prisoners' children who are the same age as their own kids.

Just as important, Angel Tree can be an effective part of your church outreach, as you build relationships with these families that last year-round.

And finally, Angel Tree Christmas is a powerful form of evangelism, as the love of Christ shines upon oft forgotten families through both the lives and the words of the volunteers. Angel Tree actively encourages gift deliverers to pray and share the gospel with the children and caregivers, and provides age-appropriate tools to help you. The intimate love of Christ is what truly attracts and transforms!

It's Not Just for Christmas Anymore

Christmas is a great time for sharing gifts and the gospel through the ministry of Angel Tree. But it's just a start. Your local Angel Tree program can change lives all year long as it helps your church create a supportive home for hurting families, where they can discover and experience the transforming power of Christ.

As a part of **Angel Tree Camping**, your church can arrange scholarships for prisoners' children to attend Christian summer camps. Angel Tree will help put you in touch with nearby camps accredited by Christian Camping International and, through the Rich and Helen DeVos scholarship fund, can help cover camping expenses.

Research shows that children benefit significantly from residential camping experiences that feature low child-to-counselor ratios and include a variety of experientially based learning opportunities. During these experiences, many children make a first-time decision to trust in Christ or deepen their commitment to him. The benefits of these camping experiences are reinforced and supplemented when local churches provide follow-up support for children returning from camp.

When it comes to having a truly significant influence in the lives of at-risk children, studies indicate that mentoring by a concerned adult is the single most effective strategy for building resiliency and curbing destructive behavior. **Angel Tree Mentoring** may be able to assist your church in starting your own mentoring program or in linking you with effective programs that already exist in your community.

Will You Help?
Your prayers and participation will help unleash God's miraculous work in the lives of prisoners and their families.

You can bring joy to prisoners' children by letting them know their mom or dad has not forgotten them.

You can give them peace by sharing Christ and inviting them to be a part of your caring church family.

You can give them a more secure future by helping their families stay strong and united, in anticipation of that day when Mom or Dad returns home.

To learn more about how you can be a part of welcoming children through Angel Tree, call us toll-free at 800-55-ANGEL or visit us at www.angeltree.org.